/—

To my friend Pat

Kurt A. Wallace

THE STATE OF NEVADA
OFFICE OF THE GOVERNOR
555 E. Washington Avenue
Suite 5100
Las Vegas, Nevada 89101

BOB MILLER
Governor

TELEPHONE
(702) 486-2500
Fax: (702) 486-2505

July 13, 1995

Kurt L. Wallach
c/o Edythe Katz
Jewish Federation of Las Vegas
3909 S. Maryland Parkway
Las Vegas, NV 89119-7520

Dear Mr. Wallach:

Having just finished reading <u>Remembering Mark</u> I wanted to take a moment to congratulate you on a moving, relevant work.

<u>Remembering Mark</u> is an outstanding tribute to the strength and resiliency of the family, demonstrating how that strength can transcend the most heinous challenges. The lessons to be learned in <u>Remembering Mark</u> are lessons that can be universally applied to all of us.

I know every parent could only hope to be so lovingly remembered, and to have such an important and meaningful legacy as that which you have created.

Again, my congratulations and my thanks.

Sincerely,

Bob Miller

BOB MILLER
Governor

REMEMBERING MARK

A BIOGRAPHY OF A FATHER

By

Kurt L. Wallach

Dedication

This book is dedicated to the memory of

the entire family of Mark Wallach

who sacrificed their lives to

Adolph Hitler's Nazis, merely in

payment for the sin of being

of the Jewish faith.

Contents

Contents
(Continued)

List of Illustrations

List of Illustrations
(Continued)

Preface

Mark Wallach, the son of very hard working small town folk living in the city of Chorostkow in the Ukraine is the subject of an unusual and prophetic-filled life which lasted for 89 years and took place in eastern Europe, western Europe and the United States of America. He was indeed a most unusual man with foresight equalled by none so far as the author knows. He married Lena Lopater at age 30 and established a family for which he cared during very trying times. His love and dedication saw them through the pre-Holocaust period as his visions of the future saved them from destruction and enabled them to lead complete lives of their own until the days of their demise.

Mark Wallach was a seer of the future and surely one of the most dedicated human beings one could ever have the privilege of knowing. He served his family well with a willingness to sacrifice all for those he loved.

His life of toil and uncertainty was never fully appreciated by those for whom he cared so very much. So much was taken for granted and many of his accomplishments were considered nothing short of routine during his lifetime. As we resurrect the past today, surely we see that was not the case at all for what was considered to be the routine and the mundane was in fact the unusual and the heroic. Few individuals portrayed their visions into the future nor had the courage to carry out the difficult deeds and tasks that needed to be done as he did.

Mark Wallach was a successful man in every way. He was loved by all who knew him, honest to the last, ambitious and industrious. We could all learn much from the manner in which he lived his life. As a husband he was second to none. The same can be said about him in his role as a loving father to his three children. He loved and respected everyone and had no enemies except the Nazis. It is indeed a shame that his wishes to bring all of his family from the Ukraine out of that dangerous zone, during World War II, were met with frustration and failure. It could never be said that he did not do all within his power to save their lives as he saved the lives of his wife's sisters, brothers-in-law and children. Greatness is rarely realized during a man's lifetime and so it was with Mark. What we see so very clearly now was blurred at the time. What successes we admire today in retrospect were seen as almost routinely habitual at the time that they occurred. It is hoped that this book will give the credit which is so long overdue him and will give the knowledge of his life to all those who read it.

Kurt L. Wallach

Forward

It is often asked, why does one write a book? I am sure that many reasons are given to this question. There are several obvious answers such as, there is an ego within the author that says, "I must write and must be known for my ability." "I must be remembered for what I have done." "This book shall be a reminder to all to know that I was here after I am gone."

Another reason that a book is often written is because the author wishes to share something of special interest to him or her with members of their society, of their family, or in the world of business, amongst their colleagues engaged in similar enterprise.

Books are written and published quite frequently by public speakers who become authors and the book provides them with additional income. Professionals will write books on their expertise. Books are often published by researchers to show, and oftentimes, to display their theories of what they have accomplished and what they wish to prove.

There are many other reasons why books are written and then published.

The question is asked, why was "REMEMBERING MARK" written? As one might defend a thesis, written for obtaining a degree, I must tell you that the book, "REMEMBERING MARK" is written in expression of true admiration for my father, whom I have, all my life, particularly after his demise, considered to be not only a wonderful man, but indeed a great man. I wrote this book in commemoration and dedication, in addition to admiration, for his being. And, lest I sound redundant in what might be read in the preface hereto, I write this in hopes that his memory will live for many years, not only amongst the family that survives him, but all those who have in one way, near or distant, been touched by his life. The trite cliche "To know him is to love him" must have been written about Mark Wallach. I am indeed proud to be his offspring.

Kurt L. Wallach

Prologue

The memories of my father, Mark and his kind and compassionate nature are the memories I carry with me from childhood. The memory that told me something about my father's strength in adversity and his commitment to what was right I learned in my adult years.

Somewhere between childhood and adulthood, a son seeks to establish his own individuality. Unfortunately, the process too often becomes one in which the son is so busy proving himself, he does not recognize what his father had to offer, nor does he let his father know how much he learned from him and loves him.

I remember when I was quite young, a fly somehow had entered the house and landed on a small side table next to where my father sat. He pulled out his handkerchief and slowly placed it to where he could drop it on the fly. Carefully gathering up the tent-like handkerchief with the fly trapped inside, he went to the door and released it. I must have had a questioning look on my face, for when he came back in, he said, "He was not hurting us, so why kill him?"

When I was still living at home in Cleveland, Mark had become quite a successful builder of luxury homes and "defense housing" units as they were called during the war. I had been talking about some of my ideas of eventually going into business for myself, although I suspected he would have liked to have me join with him. How well I remember some advice he gave me. He said, "If you always put yourself in your customers' shoes, do what is best for them, and make sure they know you have their interests at heart, you will find your customers will be the best advertising for you that you could possibly have. They know they will get a quality job, one that in the end eventually will give them the fewest troubles, and that you will stand behind it if there are problems for which you are responsible. Nobody has had to take me to court to have me correct any problems for which I am responsible." There were those who spoke with admiration of my father's integrity. One of his clients once said, if somewhat facetiously, "Your Dad would come in and personally replace a light bulb if it did not last as long as it should!"

I learned much from my father and my memories of him mean so much to me. I wish I could let him know how important he was to me and what a strong impact he had on my life. Most sons probably have the same feelings for their fathers. My Dad is no longer with us in this life, but he remains a part of who and what I am.

As my father's descendants read this story and as I recount some of our family's heritage, I hope they will inherit a sense of belonging, a sense of bonding to my father's memory. If it also gives the reader a greater understanding of how we all have been shaped by a complex past and should, therefore, acknowledge Mark's role in helping to mold us, I will be twice rewarded.

The story of Mark Wallach's life involves much more than just those years in which he lived. His life was strongly influenced by the unique circumstances of historical factors. We will look at these as our story progresses.

PROLOGUE

*   *   *

Over the centuries, as Jews, his ancestors had to contend with and adapt to more than the normal variations of life. Such inheritance made it necessary to develop strength of character and purpose. My Dad succeeded and became the generous and kind man I was privileged to know. To understand this, one must first understand his family's ancestry.
In pages yet to be read, allow me to trace history - far back - to enlighten and edify so that understanding Mark can be made a little easier.

CHAPTER 1

THE ROOTS

In the year 972 B.C., King David, living in the country of Canaan, now known as Israel, had two sons. They were half-brothers, Adonijah and Solomon. After the birth of Adonijah, King David married Bathsheba, and Solomon was born.

Adonijah, an officer in the Army of King David, led raids on neighboring settlements, adding territory to the Kingdom. He was a big man who excelled in sports and for whom there was no equal in swordsmanship and military talents. Taking power and territory by force was in his nature. He often would ridicule Solomon, accusing him of using intrigue and twisted interpretations of the law to obtain his ends.

Adonijah was idolized by his troops and

favored in the court for his conquests that brought new wealth to the Kingdom. His brash and forceful personality made him popular with everyone. Solomon's jealousy turned into burning hatred by Adonijah's jibes of "Solomon the politician," a hatred he was careful not to display, which led him to plot against the brother who stood in the way of his ultimate ambitions. In the Jewish culture, the eldest son was the inheritor of all. Solomon fervently wanted to be head of the Kingdom once his father, David, died.

To insure that he would become the inheritor, Solomon plotted the murder of Adonijah and carried it out. He and his followers hunted down as many of the royal heirs of Adonijah as they could find in order to prevent the restoration of the legitimate line. Some of Adonijah's successors managed to escape to Egypt. Their successors moved even further West, over the mountains to what is now Morocco and Algeria, where the Berbers gave them sanctuary.

Having been descended from the line of Adonijah, son of King David, there has never been anyone in the Wallach dynasty named Solomon. Family history recounts that whenever the name of Solomon was mentioned, members of the Wallach family would mouth, "murderer."

Berbers were essentially farmers, living in small, loosely joined villages. The Berber culture has been traced as far back as 2400 B.C. when these tribes formed the states of Mauritania and Numidia, which later became Morocco and Algeria. The Berbers had become Christians during the first century A.D., after coming under the influence of Christian apostles preaching throughout Northern Africa.

About the seventh century, the Arabs conquered many of the Berbers and the descendants of Adonijah who were largely identified with the Berbers. The descendants became a tribe known as the Dzerouah and still continued to practice a form of Judaism. Some of their history was passed on through scrolls and parchments and much by word of mouth. Since each eldest son was to inherit the position of leader of the clan, the present leader would instruct him in his future duties as well as pass on their history.

Legend says that at one time, the tribe known as the Dzerouah had not produced a male heir. It so happened that the eldest girl seemed to have inherited many of the genes of the original Adonijah. During an attack by the Arabs, it was she who had rallied the clan and convinced the Berbers it was in their interest to band together in defense of their villages. In childhood, she had joined boys in hunting and proved to have more than enough stamina to track down prey. Taller than average, this young woman demonstrated her skill in mediating family arguments and soon was sought out whenever there were difficult decisions to make. This inevitably led to the clan voting for a change in the traditional custom of the eldest son inheriting the position of leadership. It was decided that the best suited, the one who demonstrated greatest ability as chosen by a council of seniors, would be their leader as High Priestess. The name "Al Kaahena" became her title as a leader in times of war. Future generations continued to select a woman as High Priestess as well as their Al Kaahena, whenever possible a daughter of the previous Al Kaahena, or another woman if there was no daughter.

Around the 8th century A.D., further Arab attacks led to the death of the Al Kaahena, and a great loss of life. They knew many of the Arab attacks were motivated by religious differences. The Jewish faith demanded of them strong family and clan ties, and the Arabs feared this seeing it as a potential threat to them. Deciding to distance themselves from the Arabs, they moved on to the city of Coimbra, capital of medieval Portugal, arriving in about the year 900 A.D.

The Christian Kingdom of Spain began to take over control of the Iberian Peninsula. As they did, some of the old towns adopted new, more Christian-like names, and those Jews living there found it desirable to adopt the names of those Christians who had helped them, for there was already a program backed by the Spanish Kingdom to eradicate all religions that were not Catholic.

A name adopted by some of our ancestors

of those living in the Spanish town of Merida was Fuentes. Another name used by some of the Wallach ancestry who had moved to Seville, Spain, was Caro. The name Lazzaro was used by some ancestors in Seville and Salamanca. Yet another group was called Pereira by those who lived in Lugo, Coimbra and Oporto, Portugal.

Even before the infamous Spanish inquisition, there was a tremendous amount of anti-Semitism during the years of 1450 A.D. to 1480 A.D., causing many of the families to move to the Mediterranean islands of Minorca and Mallorca, where they lived until some time in the 1500's.

The Inquisition began in Spain in 1492 under Queen Isabella. Initially its main purpose was to make Spain exclusively Catholic. Many Jews converted to Catholicism to save their lives. Many did so falsely as they clandestinely continued worshipping in the Jewish faith. Many Jews and Muslims left Spain. Had they refused to become Christians, they would have been cruelly persecuted and punished. Those Jews and Muslims whom

16

they felt had been insincere in their conversion, were often murdered. This extreme and cruel intolerance continued until it was abolished in 1843. Anti-Semitism was rearing its ugly head as it had for many years before and would continue to do so for centuries to come. The Jewish people were not to live in peace then, and it seems, forever.

CHAPTER 2

AS WE LOOK BACK

During the 16th century, with the Inquisition making life intolerable, many of the forerunners of the Wallach clan left Minorca and Mallorca and moved to Rome, Italy.

One of the families that settled in Rome was the Lazzaros. David Lazzaro became a physician to the Pope, and his influential position was very helpful in rescuing other members of the Wallach family and many other Jews wanting to escape the anti-Semitism of Spain. It is said history repeats itself. As we will see in future chapters, my father was able to help many escape the horrors of the Nazi persecution of Jews. Though this occurred 300 years later, it was nevertheless a recurrence and repetition of the days of David Lazzaro. The Lazzaros and others who had adopted Spanish names continued to live in Rome. During the period in which many of the clan lived in Rome, there were several Popes, not all as understanding and as true to the Christian faith as was true in the early years.

At first, those Jews who had accepted Catholicism as a way of escaping persecution were still allowed to practice their traditional Jewish faith. The Pope realized that the Jews converted to Catholicism because they feared for their lives. He found nothing wrong with their continued practice of Judaism. He was satisfied that at least the Jews acknowledged the one true God, rather than multiple gods like so many other religions.

There were those who managed to change such Christian tolerance, and again Jews were persecuted because of their religion and were hounded into ghettos, or worse. As a result, in the 1500's and onwards, various parts of the family migrated to different areas of the Roman Empire. Some returned to the Middle East thinking of it as their homeland, while others, fearful of Arab persecution, migrated to areas of middle Europe. During the 17th century, the family was expanding rapidly, and their descendants were emigrating as far as the northern portions of the Roman Empire, the little Germanic states, the Netherlands, and to what is now Austria.

Most of these immigrants lived together in ghettos and reverted to the Hebrew names they had when they lived with the Berbers and inherited from when living in Canaan.

Those who migrated to the area of Wallachia, a province of Romania, avoided the royal cities and accepted offers by noblemen to settle on their estates. They managed the estates for the noblemen and were provided with land and homes. This also involved their collecting of rents from leaseholders on the land, and when turned over to the noblemen, they were given a commission.

Over the years they grew prosperous, and many of the noblemen relinquished all duties to their estates, depending on their Jewish managers since they were occupied with either fighting small wars, leading expensive social lives, gambling, and mismanaging whatever monies they had. The strong, unifying ties of the Jewish faith gave these estate managers the strength enjoyed in today's larger corporations, where they could draw on each other and take risks otherwise prohibitive. When the noblemen were short of funds, they found they could borrow from the Jews who were managing their estates. When their debts became more than they could repay, the noblemen found ways of blaming the Jews for their plight. Inevitably, this led to renewed persecution of the Jews, and over the years they were driven back into ghettos.

During the reign of Maria Theresa, the Austrian Archduchess (1740-1780), many Jews were conscripted into the army to defend Austria against Napoleon Bonaparte. In order to make it easier for the authorities, new names were given to families. In the late 1700's, the clans of our family were given Germanic names. These were Fell, Mantel, Winter, Burstein and Wallach. The name Wallach was given most likely because they had come from Wallachia, a part of Romania, still so known today.

CHAPTER 3

CHOROSTKOW

It was a cold morning on March 1, 1892, when Clara Winter Wallach was lying near the midwife who stood over her as a screaming baby came out of her womb. It was a healthy boy to be named Mark, son of David Eli and Clara Winter Wallach. The semi-rural community in which this birth took place was in the town of Chorostkow, located on the border of the river Tajne between Husiatyn and Kopyczynce. The territory is located approximately 30 miles south southeast of Tarnopol in a very fertile area known as Podolya Galicia. This land is now a part of the Ukraine. Before 1772, the town was Polish. In 1772, together with the rest of Galicia, it was passed down to Austria-Hungary which controlled it until after World War I. From 1919 to 1945, Chorostkow was again Polish. It became Russian once again in

1945 after the Great War. From a decree that was published by Cardinal Nicholas Vizitsky in 1748, we learned that an independent prefecture existed in Chorostkow as early at the 17th Century. To this belonged the small villages of Chlopowka, Greater Howilow, Lesser Howilow, Karaszynce, Kluwince, Peremilow, Uwisla, Meszczawa and Wierchowca.

In the middle of the 18th century, the owner of the domain, Count Sieminski, granted to the village the rights of a town but reserved to himself certain privileges of the province. In order to develop the town, which was Mark's birthplace and my roots, he invited Artisans and other Jewish businessmen from the towns of Galicia and granted them the right to live as a separate Jewish community from the economic and social points of view. This was, in fact, a ghetto. Unlike a modern state which guarantees every citizen residents' rights, each prince, duke, state or city owner, during the Middle Ages as well, had the sovereign right to admit or exclude people. The Jews coming to Poland in the Middle Ages and after, received residents' rights from these magnets that exempted them from city jurisdiction and taxation and gave them a kind of extra territorial status. The magnets offered incentives to Jews in order to avail themselves of Jewish entrepreneurial skills needed to develop the territory.

An independent community and independent cemetery for the Jews did not exist at this time. The first group of Jews that came from Podolya in the middle 18th century was only four in number and was headed by Jacob Pepper. Sieminski, who owned the town, invited them to help build the community which was intended to serve as a commercial center for many farms. It was to be a place where Count Sieminski could sell his crops. According to Polish law, Sieminski could build houses for the Jews. He nominated Pepper, a tough, energetic man, to be the town manager. Pepper leased the province from Sieminski.

Thanks to Pepper's considerable initiative, the population of the community slowly increased. According to a census held in February 1765, there were now 42 Jewish tax payers and two infants. In the whole district of Trembowle, there were a total of 7,534 Jews. There were approximately 132,000 Jews living in the entire Ukraine. Mark Wallach was to be born into this arena many years later.

At the end of the 18th century, Chorostkow gained recognition as a community unit, though not as yet an independent community. Thanks to Jacob Pepper, Count Sieminski helped the Jews build their great synagogue where they later established a Talmudic school. Later on they established a tailors' guild. Eventually, the Austrian authorities began to harass the little Jewish commonwealth and in 1785, they claimed the synagogue had been constructed without a license from the government. Vienna issued a directive that those responsible for the construction of this synagogue should be punished and the building torn down.

The majority of Jews were small businessmen, retailers, and peddlers who worked in surrounding towns. With the money they earned from their businesses, they bought agricultural products from the farmers. There were also a substantial number of Jewish Artisans, mainly tailors who worked for Jewish and non-Jewish customers alike, some of whom traveled from village to village to mend clothes. They often received food in exchange for their services, and they would subsequently sell the food in town. In the days of the Austrians, the Jews achieved distinction in wood and forestry products. These were sold mainly in the town of Danzig, which is now known Gdansk. The first Rabbi known to be among the Chorostkow Jews was David Solomon Abschutz who was a follower of the Rabbi of Czortkow. Rabbi Abschutz helped to establish the burial society. He and Rabbi Javis of Kopyczynce were given broad authority to establish rules to apply to regulate social life in Chorostkow.

During the Austrian rule, the fate of the Chorostkow Community was similar to that of other Jewish Communities in Galicia with regard to taxes and social situations. Between 1772 and 1848, Galician Jews suffered greatly under various laws enacted against them by the Austrian Monarchs and their governments.

Empress Maria Theresa was a bigoted Catholic and even her son, Emperor Joseph II, who was somewhat more enlightened, considered Jews harmful to the state. His edict of a sort of mild tolerance was based on the idea of reforming the Jews and making them more useful to the state. But the effort to assimilate Jews had its price. Jews would have to sacrifice their national religious culture. The autonomy of the community, the rabbinical court, and craftsmen's skills were abolished to attain the goal. Jews were expelled from some villages and various types of professions were prohibited to them. They were also subjected to special taxes for their protection and toleration as well as taxes on their property, employment, and marriages. After 1789, the Jews were included in obligatory military service, forced to adopt German names, and their children were compelled to attend government sponsored schools.

The revolution of 1848 and the arrival of Emperor Franz Joseph improved things considerably. The French Revolution was a popular uprising through all of the countries in Europe. Liberal and Socialists led the peoples protest against the tyranny of European rulers. The success of the February Revolution in France encouraged uprising elsewhere including Austria. Vienna rose against the absolute Chancellor, Prince Metternich, and forced him to flee the country. Emperor Ferdinand of Austria was compelled to abdicate and was succeeded by Emperor Franz Joseph who adopted very liberal policies. Galician Jews fought with the revolutionaries and lent considerable support to Franz Joseph whom they considered a benevolent monarch.

Under Franz Joseph, special taxes on Jews were rescinded and, ultimately, most restrictions were lifted. Galician Jews entered political life, and many Jews flocked to Vienna. Economic life also improved for the Galician Jews at that time. Rich Jews were entering banking, import, export and oil industry trades but for many, the economic situation continued with only slight improvement.

In 1848, the Cossacks, sent by Czar Nicholas I to Austria to fight against Hungary, passed through Chorostkow. While western

Europe was in the throes of liberalizing, the Revolution of 1848 in Russia, under Nicholas I, was absolutist and intent upon suppression of all kinds of revolutionary movements. In default of such movement in Russia itself, Russian hostility found an outlet in a punitive expedition sent to support the Austrians in the pacification of mutinous Hungary. In 1860, there was a cholera epidemic in Husiatyn and some neighboring towns. Also in 1860, a rumor spread that the Austrian government was about to forbid marriage to all males under the age of 24. Most of the youth in Chorostkow between the ages of 14 and 16 (and even younger girls) entered into quick marriages without considering status or fortune.

On June 7, 1862, a big fire caused major damage to Jewish property in the town. Fifty large houses as well as many stores and a prayer place were burned. Another fire in 1869 caused great damage to the town from which the inhabitants were unable to salvage very much. Again the Jews were helped by neighboring communities as well as by the owner of the town who contributed money as

The Town of Chorostkow 1875

well as all kinds of materials including not only wood, sand, and bricks to build houses but also flour and other food stuff.

In 1893, a Catholic convocation in Cracow proclaimed an economic boycott against Jews. In 1900, Poles and Ukrainians combined to exclude Jews from merchandising of agricultural produce. The boycott and economic pressure impoverished the masses of Jews in Galicia. A total of 236,000 Jews emigrated from Galicia between 1881 and 1919. Many came to America. The Wallach family left Chorostkow and went to Budapest. Young Mark, at age 3, along with his brothers and sister escaped to Hungary for three years, after which David Eli and Clara felt it was safe enough to return to Chorostkow in 1898. Slightly after their return two of his older brothers, Joseph and Adolph, emigrated to the United States. Adolph, the first to leave, said his goodbyes in 1900, never again to see his family except for Mark and Joseph, who left Chorostkow six years later joining Adolph in 1906 in Cleveland, Ohio. The family had been split into two parts.

At the outbreak of World War I, tens of thousands of Jews fled to Hungary, Bohemia, and Vienna. During the Russian occupation of Galicia, the Jews who remained suffered greatly. In the internal life of the Chorostkow community, there were not many changes, except the strengthening of the Hasidic movement in the first half of the 19th century. Hasidism was a religious and social movement that spread throughout the Jewish communities of eastern Europe in the middle 18th century. Founded by Rabbi Eliazar, the Hasidism emphasized worshiping God through joy and had strong, cabalistic inclinations. The rapid spread of Hasidism met with severe opposition from wide circles known as Mitnaggedim which, in Hebrew, meant "the opposer," who thought the Hasidim were rowdy and frivolous. In Chorostkow, many Rabbis were followers of the Hasidic movement, and Hasidic congregations formed there in Husiatyn as well as Czortkow.

Throughout the second half of the 19th century until the beginning of the first World War in 1914, the economic situation of Jewish population was tolerable. Chorostkow held a

"Fair Day" or market day each Monday to which people from the surrounding villages came. They sold their products including poultry, eggs, meat, horses and the like. There in Jewish stores they bought such necessities as they required. These fairs provided a major source of revenue for the Jews. Maurice Samuel, in the World of Sholom Aleichem, (pages 26 to 27) describes a typical East European shtetl (small town). "A jumble of houses clustered higgledy-piggledy about a market place as crowded as a slum. The streets are as tortuous as a Talmudic argument. They are bent into question marks and folded into parentheses. They run into cul-de-sacs like a theory arrested by a fact; they ooze off into lanes, alleys, backyards... At the center is the marketplace, with its shops, booths, tables, stands, butcher blocks... The tumult of the marketplace is one of the wonders of the world." This could well have been a reasonably accurate description of the town of Chorostkow.

As of the last quarter of the 19th century, the occupations of the Jewish residents of Chorostkow were various. Out of 358 families, five heads of family were engaged in finance of which David Eli Wallach was one, 176 were businessmen, of which David Eli Wallach was also one, 16 were engaged in a sort of hotel/cafe/restaurant type trade, 12 were farmers, 83 were artisans, 14 were synagogue officials, 16 were in some sort of transportation-related activity, 20 were teachers, 8 were dealers of various sorts, 5 were porters, and 3 were in paramedical occupations.

Of the 176 families in business, five were involved in flour milling. Of the five in finance, there was one banker, one rent collector, two landowners and one person described as the richest man in town, again possibly this may have been David Eli Wallach, who not only sold the farm equipment machinery to the farmers, but also had great holdings in finance having financed lands for Barons turned playboys who squandered their fortunes. Much land was held by David Eli and he might very well have been the richest Jew in the community. There was one doctor and one pharmacist, as well as one midwife.

Out of the 14 religious officials, there was one Rabbi, three cantors, one kosher butcher, one scribe, and three judges. Despite the fact that Chorostkow was located in a remote corner of the Podolya district of Galicia and thus subject to the strong influence of the great religious Rabbis, nevertheless, modern ideas took hold as early as 1860.

The Jewish Enlightenment had its beginning in Prussia. Moses Mendelssohn (1792 to 1886), the father of Felix Mendelssohn, the great composer, was its founder. This movement to spread modern European culture among Jews was in reality an off-shoot of the general enlightenment in Western Europe during the 18th century. The French Revolution, the Industrial Revolution, and capitalism stirred critical thoughts about all prior classes and group relationships. Jews with liberal ideas became convinced that cultural assimilation with the Christian environment would establish their social acceptance once and for all. Great emphasis was placed by Mendelssohn and his circle on displacing Yiddish, a corrupt jargon, with German, although the Hebrew tongue continued to be regarded as sacrosanct. Eventually Moses Mendelssohn left Judaism altogether and when Felix the great composer was born, he was to be born a non-Jew. Although of Jewish background, Felix Mendelssohn never acknowledged the fact that his father, Moses, had been one of the most heard voices in the Jewish community prior to his birth.

From Berlin, the Jewish Enlightenment spread quickly to Galicia. It was really a form of modern reform Judaism. Tarnopol, the largest city near Chorostkow, was greatly influenced by the movement. Jewish schools having German as the language of instruction were instituted there as were "reform" synagogues. Followers of the Enlightenment (maskillim) launched vitriolic attacks on ritual-obsessed, orthodox Jewish fanatics but reserved their strongest fire for the Hasidim and their uninhibited Jewish emotionalism. The Haskalah Age did not bring about Jewish emancipation. The Russian pogroms of 1881 are a clear reminder of that but the Haskalah gave organization and direction to the aspirations of modern thinking Jews just emerging from the ghetto confinement. It also played a vital part in the Jewish struggle for civil emancipation and caused many Jews to come to terms with their unique identity in the context of Western culture.

As one of the first modern Jews in the town, Rabbi Kohanka was a very pious and scholarly Jew. He was a tailor by profession and was open to ideas outside the Jewish tradition. The Rabbi loved studying the Hebrew scriptures and the Talmud (the name given to each of two collections of records of the discussion and administration of Jewish law by scholars and jurists in various academies during the period of 200 to 500) and read the book of fables as commented on by Mendelssohn. He had considerable influence on the youth of Chorostkow who began to study Hebrew as well as German.

Another modern Jew was Rabbi David Labe Harnish. Also very pious and a great scholar. He spoke Hebrew fluently, was widely knowledgeable, and well-read in German and Hebrew literature. His house was a place for modern Jews of the town to meet and discuss the meaning of difficult passages of the bible, the modern Hebrew language, and such German authors as Schiller and Goethe.

It was through the youth who had been exposed to non-traditional learning that the idea of Zionism began to infiltrate Chorostkow. Zionism was the movement to secure the Jewish return to Israel that had, until the 19th century, always been a part of traditional liturgy and occasionally surfaced in the various movements and numerous individual immigrations. The term took on specific meaning in the late 19th century, especially among Jews in Eastern Europe, i.e., it referred to the encouragement of migration of Jews to Palestine and the founding of settlements there. Rabbi Hirzl, one of the prime movers of Zionism who had witnessed the violent anti-Semitism in France while covering the first Dreyfuss Trial as a journalist, was a modern (reform) Jew.

One of the first advocates of the Zionist idea was Hayim Fraysh, who lived from 1875 to 1923. He was a clock maker by profession, a very educated man, who, together with metal worker Jacob Berman, established the first Zionist society in the early 20th century in Chorostkow. The City Council of Chorostkow had 18 members of whom six were Jewish, six Polish, and six Ruthenian. As of 1870, there was only one doctor in the town, Dr. Orhahan from Tarnopol. From 1920 to 1941, the doctor was Dr. Vishnobitzer, also from Tarnopol. There were several organizations in the town of Chorostkow. An association of artisans was founded in 1875. There was also a women's organization founded by Mrs. Cecelia Rath.

From 1765 to 1880, the Jewish population grew from 42 persons to 2,130, an increase of 475%. Between 1880 and 1900, the population decreased from 2,130 to 2,075, a drop of 2.3%. The general population, by way of contrast, grew from 3,493 in 1880 to 6,261 in the year 1900, a 79% increase. In 1910, there were 1,871 Jews, representing 204 or nearly 10% fewer than in 1900. The general population increased from 6,261 to 6,498 in the same decade.

America undoubtedly was a primary lure

for Jews from Chorostkow at that time, as it was for Eastern European Jews in general. There had been a trickle of Jewish immigration to America from Europe before 1880, a total 7,500 Jewish immigrants in the years between 1820 and 1870, and more than 40,000 in the 1870's. The Russian pogroms of the early 1880's spurred massive immigrations to America for which Galicia and Austria, and, in particular, Vienna were way stations. While many Jews came to America to escape persecution, others came for reasons of personal relief including avoidance of military service, though such pressures were not new to the Jews. In America, they had, for the first time, some place else to go, a new world perceived as radically different from the one in which they lived. Avoidance of military service not too much later, was one of the causes which mandated Mark to leave Chorostkow.

Mark's life in his little "shtetl" was one of both joys and hardships. The joys were mostly that of a young boy growing up, partaking of the daily learning processes, laughing, playing and joking as all children do.

His demeanor was generally one of happiness, although the pogroms and persecution of the Jews trickled down even to the small child who was fully cognizant that major problems were often at hand. His mother and dad lived in fear many times. Their possessions and worldly goods were always at great risk and little Mark was aware of this. Running from the Cossacks and fearing them was a regular event. When would another decree be ordered? When would there be another raid? When would they ride through town again killing the chickens, shooting some cows, burning a barn here and there, beating up some Jews and generally terrorizing the population? These were the fears with which Mark grew up. And these were the fears which matured him and gave him a greater insight than would normally be the case for a growing young boy.

It is my belief that never in his growing up years did he really believe that he would stay in Chorostkow and live a life of fear not knowing what would be next. When there was peace, there was financial comfort. When terror reigned, as it did many times, more was at stake than for most. His life could surely not have been compared to a small boy growing up under what we might consider normal circumstances in this day and age. Mark learned early of good and evil. He learned of kindness and of terror. He learned early enough to be grateful when there was peace.

The lives of David Eli and Clara had made them well accustomed to the hardships and fears which were often just around the corner. The rumors, the suspecting, and the unsureness of life in Chorostkow for this family was not an easy road to travel.

Despite the difficulties, Mark was a well adjusted child. He had made many friends and was constantly into some kind of childish mischief. School was a chore, but it offered many friends and opportunities for play. Mark enjoyed both and grew up with visions for the future which would hold big things for him. Maybe he would travel to America one day like his brother, A.T. Maybe he would become famous. Maybe great, yet to be imagined wonderful things would happen to him. Living with great anticipation and imagination, Mark was generally a very happy child and despite all, quite normal.

CHAPTER 4

TARNOPOL

The city of Tarnopol is located in the province of Lviv in eastern Galicia, at this time the Ukraine. It is the closest "large" city to Chorostkow.

Jews began to settle in the city shortly after its foundation in 1540. An organized community had already formed before 1648. Jews took an active part in the defense of the city during the many attacks to which it had been subjected in the mid 17th century. The royal grant authorizing the erection of a fortified synagogue already constructed by this time, stipulated that the community was to install artillery loopholes on all sides and to acquire cannons. The members of the community, among whom artisans were singled out, were required to defend the synagogue under the direction of a "Jewish hetmann."

During the attacks of Bohdan Chmielnicki, a Ukrainian nationalist and Cossack leader, however, most of the Jews fled and those who remained were massacred.

Privileges were renewed in 1740 allowing the Jews of Tarnopol to live in and conduct trade in any part of the city. Jews were permitted to purvey alcoholic liquor and to keep taverns. Jewish artisans could engage in crafts, provided that they observed the rules of the Christian guilds and paid a specified sum to the guild funds. The Tarnopol community built up a flourishing economy, controlling the grain and cattle trade. It also played an important role in Jewish autonomy in the 18th century. Noted rabbis of Tarnopol of this period included Joshua Heshel Babad, who was dismissed from the rabbinate in 1718 and returned to the office in 1724. He was followed by Jacob Isaac Landow, in office until 1777. The position of the Jewish community deteriorated after Tarnopol passed to Austria in 1772. Taxation became increasingly burdensome. The census for 1788 registered 6,380 Jewish males and 6,374 females from the district of Tarnopol, including eight subsidiary communities. The Jews were mainly occupied as taverners and retailers with a considerable number of artisans.

Tarnopol Jews suffered severely during World War I as the city changed hands seven times in the fighting. With the dissolution of the Hapsburg monarchy, a Ukrainian government was organized in Tarnopol and in December, 1918, a Jewish militia of 800 men was formed. In the election to the Jewish national council in western Ukraine held in March 1919, the Zionists won a clear majority. The council was active until Tarnopol was taken by the Poles, who encouraged Polish assimilationists within the community and turned over the leadership to them. The last head of the Tarnopol Jewish community was the Zionists leader, Zvi Parnas. By 1939 there were 18,500 Jews in Tarnopol.

During the Holocaust period, as in other communities under Soviet occupation (1939 - 1941), the Jewish community organizations were dissolved, political parties prohibited, Hebrew education discontinued, and the

Yiddish schools nationalized. A very short time after the outbreak of the German - Soviet war (June 1941) Tarnopol was occupied by the German Army. 5,000 Jews were massacred between July 4-11, 1941. After a few days 63 Jews belonging to the intelligentsia were invited to the Gestapo on the pretext of receiving public appointments, but were all murdered in the Gestapo office. Ukrainian militia was quite a help in this action as well as in others. A ghetto was established in Tarnopol in September 1941 and was the first to be set up in Galicia. Herman Mueller, commandant of the Geheime Staats Polizei (Gestapo) in the Tarnopol district was sentenced to death after the war for his activity in Tarnopol.

In the ghetto over 12,500 people were crowded into a small area. Attempts were made to renew their Jewish school system and several orphanages and old age homes were established. At that time the ghetto inmates were gradually murdered. On March 25, 1942 1,000 Jews were shot on the streets and the nearby forests. Thousands of Jews were seized in the streets or taken from their homes for forced labor at labor camps in the Tarnopol district. Between August 29 and 31, 1942 over 4,000 Jews from Tarnopol were sent to the Belzec Death camp. On September 30, 1942 a further 1,000 Jews were sent there. On April 18, 1943 in the last action, 2,000 Jews were killed near Tarnopol.

In December 1944 S.S. Officer Richard Rokita (who survived the war and was later ferreted out by Simon Wiesenthal) was apprehended and died in prison before judgment was handed down. He had organized a labor camp (Rokitalager). The camp numbered about 800 men and women in various German installations outside the camp. On the big action day (aktion tag), July 23, 1943, the labor camp was liquidated. In August 1943 Tarnopol was declared "judenrein" (free of Jews).

Inside the Rokitalager a clandestine resistance cell comprised of members of Zionist youth movements was organized under the leadership of Joseph Blumenfeld who kept in touch with Russian partisans. During the last days of the occupation he was forced to

The City of Tarnopol 1877

come out of hiding, was recognized by the Germans and was shot to death. A prisoner of the camp and activist of the underground cell Anna Federbusch-Ophir, survived the war, and later gave evidence of the happenings in the Tarnopol ghetto and at the Rokita labor camp.

The cooperation with the Russian partisans terminated when they left the area of the underground cell and most of the members were killed during the liquidation. When the Red Army recaptured Tarnopol in the spring of 1944, about 150 Jews came out of hiding and 200 returned to the city from the Soviet Union where they had spent the war years, some of them as soldiers in the Soviet Army. In the late 1960's there lived about 500 Jews in Tarnopol.

A monument was erected on the site of the two last executions, to the memory of the Jewish martyrs of the Holocaust. This monument was completely destroyed in the 1950's. Only a heap of stones remains there today. The old Jewish cemetery of Tarnopol was converted into a building site and the grounds of two other cemeteries came to house nine garages.

The city of Tarnopol was to become the graveyard for Mark's brothers, sisters-in-law, nieces and nephews. His eldest, and most beloved brother, Moses, as well as his brother Isaac, nicknamed "Itchoe," had come to Tarnopol years before. The nieces and nephews, all of them, are buried somewhere in this old town. The human tragedies of the times through anti-Semitism, from the Ukrainians, whose anti-Semitic antics were not much less than the Nazis, saw to it that the Wallach clan that remained in this part of the world was not to be, as they were all shot and murdered, to the very last one.

Mark's memories of the old world, as he on so many occasions expressed them, were not only of Chorostkow, his home, but extended to Tarnopol. It was here that hope lie in his youth, and tragedy in later years. Today, all that exists is memories and even those have faded into the far distance amongst the living members of the Wallach family. As I write this tragic account, I ponder and I wonder how many of the young and modern

TARNOPOL

Wallach generation know of the Chorostkow-Tarnopol history and the calamity, terror, disaster, and catastrophe of it. The murders of at least half the Wallach clan is recorded here and must not be forgotten.

CHAPTER 5

YOUNG MARK

The following are selections from an autobiography of a man named Pinchas Sherlag. The title of his work is called "In A Poor Town." The town is Chorostkow.

The author was born in 1856. Among the things he writes about (he writes mostly about himself) are superstitions that his family held.

"At school, children hear terrible stories about all kinds of devils. One told of a man who was wandering around the town in the middle of the night. A devil in a great black coat, with a cylinder on his head, followed him and frightened him."

"There was also an old house near the synagogue, where people believe the devil used to work his evil and tricks. Stories were also told about babies who died on the first day of their lives, because some kind of devil passed near their house. In order to ward off the evil spirits, the people used to take pieces of paper, containing chapters of Biblical verse, and hang them on the wall near the mother's bed. Sometimes the messages contained the names of angels, or for girls, a picture of a half circle was drawn (for boys something else was drawn). People believed that, after death, some individuals were rejected by the earth and condemned to wander for the rest of their existence through forests and deserts. Witnesses were prepared to testify that they had seen such living dead walking among the townspeople of Chorostkow."

"Once a very famous Rabbi visited Chorostkow while Galicia was in the middle of a very bad cholera epidemic. Many people had left the area, to go to places where the epidemic had either already been or had not yet arrived. Once the epidemic left Chorostkow, other people started to come to town to live there. Among them was the famous Rabbi, who arrived with some of his the biggest apartment in town where he used to live and eat with a very wealthy man, Mr. Keller. As word got around that the Rabbi was there, people came from all over to see him. As a result, there was much bustle and activity during the several weeks that he stayed here. People came over with presents and messages, asking the Rabbi to help them."

"Every Saturday, after morning prayer, there was a big breakfast. Tables were set for hundreds of guests. Curious people often pushed and shoved each other to gain a vantage point from which to see the great Rabbi. On one Saturday, I was fortunate enough to get into the big room and see the Rabbi, who was surrounded by his senior-most followers first, with others arrayed at a distance. He took his place at the head of the table and began to drink his soup. When he pushed the bowl away, many of his followers scrambled to touch and taste his soup. This sideshow went on, when the Rabbi was served with meat, and with other courses of the meal." And so the story went. Such folklore was not uncommon during these times. Often tales more far-fetched were told and just as often the ridiculous and sublime were accepted as the truth. Education was sorely needed.

In 1869, a huge fire swept the town, leaving nothing but stones and dust. After that, even the dust was swept away by a giant storm. Many people were shocked and fled the town. The fire burned the whole day and night and barred any access to the community. For 24 hours, people had to stay outside of town, weeping and worrying about relatives, who they did not know were dead or alive. The following day saw how terrible the disaster had been. Nothing was left of the houses, people were without food or clothing, suffering from the cold of the night. Some were able to go to relatives' homes, which, though completely destroyed, did provide some shelter from the cold. Almost immediately thereafter, people began to build new houses. The Count of the town, Count Livitsky, who was a very good and generous man, gave a large amount of money and food and gave building materials such as wood, stone, and sand to every person who was willing to rebuild his house. Everyone was pleased by the Count's generosity. Many were thus able to rebuild their homes.

Mark Wallach, as a young man, lived through much Chorostkow history that had caused profound changes in attitudes in both governments and individuals. His ancestry experienced more than most of us. Hardships built strength as well as consideration of others, opportunities for learning and material success created wisdom and tolerance. Chorostkow obviously was not the most worldly place in which Mark could learn the ways of mankind. The family having emigrated from Galicia, eventually resolved this. My father was able to trace his ancestry back as early as the 1700's to his great-grandparents, Isaac and Sophia and their son, Benesh, who had eight children. One of these was David Eli Wallach, the father of Mark, born in 1850. David Eli had married Clara Winter in 1870. Their sixth son was Mark, my father, born on March 1, 1892. At least Mark claimed that he was born on March 1 because it was a Leap Year and possibly he arrived February 29. The family joke was that he was actually born on the 29th of February. Not wanting to celebrate his birthday only once every four years and being denied gifts every year, he changed the date.

The maintenance of the family unit was much more important in those days than it seems to be today and this was particularly true of Mark's family. Mobility nevertheless became reality and could not be denied. It had become obvious to many members of the family that the real opportunity for a better life lay in the city of Tarnopol or overseas, rather than in Chorostkow and thus Moses and "Itchoe" moved and sought their fortunes in Tarnopol. In 1900, at the age of 21, Mark's older brother, A.T., (Adolf Tobias) left Chorostkow for the United States passing through Ellis Island and from there to Cleveland, Ohio. Six years later, he was followed there by another brother, Samuel Joseph, who was six years older than Mark. The rest of the family remained in Tarnopol and Chorostkow.

During this period, Galicia was a German speaking part of Austria-Hungary, rather than Polish-speaking, although it had been Polish

Dynasty had mandated German to be the official language, but there was, nevertheless, a strong movement toward Polish as the language of the region. The early years of Mark's life were problem filled living in Chorostkow, as he and his family lived in what was called a "shtetl" or village, a small town where living conditions were not much more than tolerable. The means of transportation was horses and horse-drawn carts traveling over muddy roads. Milk was delivered in its original container from the cow since the cows were driven down the street and often milked there. Milk, freshly obtained from the cow, was poured from small wooden pails into whatever household container was presented by the woman of the house. Backyards and open lots often harbored chickens and cows, and piles of hay for horses were stacked in small shelters.

Mark's father, David Eli, was a man in business, distributing farm machinery both new and used. He was also heavily involved in the money lending business. He certainly would have been considered an important member of the community. His vast land holdings were

obtained through forfeited collateral and that
made him, indeed, a well-off individual in the
community. He had helped his customers
finance their purchases of farm machinery that
led to some loans for other purposes as well.
I am sure some of his entrepreneurship must
have greatly influenced my father. David Eli
was not only a successful businessman and
large land holder, but he was also a very
educated man for his time, having wide
interests. One of his accomplishments was
spending his spare time over the years in
creating a perpetual calendar. He worked on
this project for almost 30 years, an indication
of the kind of tenacity inherited by my father.
I have a copy of this calendar. The work
consists of thousands, perhaps hundreds of
thousands references. This calendar can
provide the day of the week for any date for
some 500 years. I cannot vouch for the truth
of this statement, but I have been told that
there is a copy of his masterpiece in the
archives of the Vatican. Completed toward the
end of the 19th century, the calendar was
published in Lemburg, now known as the city
of Lviv. It is a great work of art. A copy of
it hung in my father and mother's home for as

long as I can remember and a copy of it has hung in my study for many years.

In spite of his position in the business community and raising a closely knit, loving family, my grandfather was still subjected to a great deal of unfair dealings and severe anti-Semitism. This was also an influence on the decision by Adolf Tobias and Samuel Joseph to leave for the New World when they each became of age. Mark, still too young, continued his schooling in Chorostkow. He was not only doing well in his studies but learning some of the more practical lessons of life as we all have. As an example, he was at one time subjected to the cruelty and abuse of a bully who often rendered him helpless due to the bully's physical strength and Mark's abhorrence of physical violence. Mark had an answer for this bully, however. My father would carry a small bag of candy as part of his school lunch and, often the bully would snatch it away from him. On one occasion, Mark considered how he could teach this bully a lesson that would end such a practice. He came up with a clever strategy, one he was sure would convince the bully that not always would the bag contain tasty candy, often licorice pellets.

One day, he put a few sheep and rabbit droppings in his bag, a variety so as to imitate the little different colored licorice pieces. As was the bully's usual habit, he tried to snatch the bag away from my father. Being prepared for this, he held on to it firmly and succeeded in foiling the first attempt. This only made the bully more determined to steal the candy. After a few attempts, my father allowed the bag to be snatched away. He told me the bully never again was anxious to steal his "candy."

I have known my father to be a very kind man and often generous to a fault. He could be firm and tenacious in accomplishing what he began but always fair and considerate of others. I believe his early experiences in life gave him much insight into adult living and instilled great maturity into the young growing boy. He had much to learn and learned fast.

YOUNG MARK

The following episode of his early childhood not only gives evidence that he had an enviable gentle nature, more than most children, but it resulted in his family giving him a nickname that lasted through his adult years.

When only five years of age Mark disappeared and his family was extremely upset at his disappearance. They scoured the neighborhood well into the night. They thought he might be in the house of a friend. His teacher reported he had been in school and had left at the usual time and it did not appear that anything was wrong. Finally the late hours made further searching impossible, and it was not until the next morning that he was thankfully found in some nearby woods asleep and cradling a small kitten. The kitten was lost and its meowing had caused my father to go in the woods to find it. As darkness approached, he became disoriented and lost. He lay down with the kitten tucked inside his jacket and slept through the night under an old hickory tree next to a brook, not waking up until the next morning. He had cats in his home that he treated as family members of the household and assumed the responsibility of their care.

The volunteer searchers that found him gave him the name of "Kotek" the Polish word for cat. As he grew older, this nickname stuck. Even his wife, Lena, would use the term endearingly with the diminutive for it, "Kotju." He had this name to his dying day.

Mark grew up speaking German but also learned Polish. When he prepared to enter into his manhood, he learned Hebrew that was a necessary part of the traditional ceremony of the bar mitzvah. As my father matured, he became more aware of the limitations of small towns such as Chorostkow. He often thought of leaving for better fields of endeavor although there was the family business into which he would one day enter. He did not hesitate making the decision to broaden his horizons and leave for greener pastures. He worked for his father and his farm machinery distribution business for a period of time. Although I never heard him complain about that, I feel that his ambitions made it difficult to remain in a business where the weight of parental authority had to be considered in all business decisions. Love of father and career ambitions were not always compatible. In addition, his father practiced his religion in a far more orthodox fashion than was true of Mark's desires. Overall, he had to test his own abilities in the competitive world. It was such considerations that led him to follow the actions of his older brothers. In 1913, at the age of 21, he left the nest. It was difficult to leave home. His father knew his son had the same kind of itch that had motivated him. The political unrest might lead not only to war but could cause an increase in an unthinking, fearful reaction of blaming Jews. Political unrest often created by those seeking to increase their own positions of power was further reason for seeking a more stable country. Being fluent in German, he moved to Magdeburg where he took a first step in establishing a clothing store. Magdeburg was a city of 250,000 within 75 kilometers of Berlin.

When it became obvious to him World War I was imminent, he moved to Holland which was expected to be neutral. There was no desire for a stint in the military and surely fighting in a war for Germany was not one of his desires. He traveled to the Hague searching for a means of supporting himself without having to call on his parents whom he felt had enough problems of their own. He eventually located a position as a wine steward in a coastal suburb of the Hague in the upper-class hotel, known as "The Kurhaus." This was becoming the premier summer resort for wealthy Europeans visiting the sea town of Scheveningen. Mark's broad cultural background served him well, earning him the reputation among the guests that Mark could be depended on to ensure that their meals were properly accented with the best choice of wines. It was remarkable for a young man of 21. His work with his father had matured him beyond his years and his instinctual desire to excel in what he did no doubt largely overshadowed his youth. I feel that many of his future successes were due to the lessons he learned from the importance of satisfying a wide variety of customers at this early age. Scheveningen, a suburb of the Hague, was to be home to the young bachelor through four years of World War I, to be viewed from a safe distance.

YOUNG MARK

Soon after the war, Mark returned to Magdeburg and reopened his clothing store, which he had voluntarily retired years before. He did well, in spite of the hard economic times caused by the Germans having lost the war. He realized that if he were to build a business that was more than a mild success, it would be necessary to have a higher quality line of goods in order to compete with some of the more established enterprises. Inflation had run rampant. Bushel baskets were more valuable than the money that filled them. Shoes cost countless billions of marks and a loaf of bread was valued at several million marks in Germany at the time. He decided that he would add a line of leather goods to the store which was located on the main street in Magdeburg. This was a wise choice and the store was successful from the onset.

Mark made what was to be a short trip to Vienna to visit his brother, Moses. While there, he met Lena Lopater and after what was an almost immediate love match, they were married in Vienna on December 3, 1922. Perhaps the emotional turmoil of falling in love at first sight or an equally great love for chocolates caused him to eat almost all of the chocolates on the tram as he went to Lena's home one evening. The chocolates were, of course, a gift for Lena. My father was 30 years old when he married my mother, Lena, who was 28. My mother was born in Brezany, Galicia on October 15, 1894.

Lena's parents, Osias and Rose Lopater, had lived in New York and had returned to Galicia when Rose was pregnant with Lena. In the next chapter, I will tell you about their experiences there and how they affected my mother. Soon it was necessary for my father to return to convince Lena's sisters and the widower, father of Lena, that Magdeburg was not that far from Vienna. Their farewells were not as painful as they might have been had they known they would not be seeing each other for several years to come.

The following year their first son, Benno, was born. My father's business had been quite successful, so much so, as to allow him to make a large commitment in celebration of the happy event. He bought a sizeable apartment building, thinking of it as an investment he could some day pass on to the new born son.

Life continued on, well. Mark and Lena prospered and when the second child, Renee, was born in 1924, my father purchased another apartment complex in honor of the birth of their daughter. His personal success allowed him to purchase two more apartment complexes when I arrived on the scene in 1926. These properties and the store selling leather goods had made him a wealthy man. Were it not for Mark's almost eccentric and semi-paranoid fears for Germany and all of Europe's future under political turmoil, which he envisioned, these would have been exceptionally joyous times. Wonderful little children, abundant love, good health and a happy marriage should have been a foundation for great happiness, all of which were accentuated by total financial success and security. But this was not the case as Mark fretted about a doomsday in the making.

During these times and my growing up years later on, my dad's never-ending love for the old hometown of Chorostkow never waned. On an almost weekly basis, I heard him and mother talking about one experience or another in the old hometown where he grew up. Chorostkow was never far from Mark's mind. Most of his family, aunts, uncles, nieces and nephews remained there until their deaths in the Holocaust in 1942 and so even afterwards, although then with much sorrow, did he discuss Chorostkow. The mourning for his brothers who died there continued almost until his demise in 1981. The death of his family was at the hands of the Nazis who murdered them. In sum, the delusions of men who were powerful for a time, whom history properly classed as insane, saw "time" diluting their false values. The Hitler era and Nazi armies destroyed Chorostkow and Tarnopol along with Mark's family, and almost every Jew in the greater community.

CHAPTER 6

EARLY ON

As was true with so many Eastern
Europeans who wished to overcome the
constraints of age-old customs that made rising
from one station of life to another so very
important and yet often so difficult, Osias and
Rose Lopater emigrated to the United States in
1888.   Many immigrants did not venture
farther west than New York City. Here there
were other immigrants to whom they could
relate. They had heard of the hardships and
difficulties of trying to make their way in a
strange country. Most of the stories they had
heard were typical of what most people hear
about countries of which they know little.
Stories of Indians and the wild west made
interesting tales, and these fables were repeated
and enhanced upon while ignoring the
opportunities of successful development that
had already begun taking place further west

Osias and Rose Lopater's Engagement Picture 1889

from New York.   Nevertheless, New York was to be their home for the next few years.

The Lopaters settled there and took the only jobs they could find open to them. They worked many long hours in the sweatshops under miserable conditions.   It was not uncommon for these immigrants to be cheated out of their meager wages, and due to such reduced incomes, living quarters were often times less than basic. The Lopaters were no different from thousands of other immigrants who suffered miserable living conditions. This type of living caused them to miss their homeland that, though a stricter and more old-fashioned way of life, was certainly far more acceptable than the living and working conditions of New York. Both Lopaters were educated and appreciative of the many fine things that they had enjoyed in Vienna which was known for its fine universities, music halls, opera, and medical achievements.

While Osias and Rose Lopater, my mother's parents, were living in New York, their daughter, Jetty, was born in 1892. Remembering their life in Vienna, they

Rose, Jetty, Young Son and Osias
New York 1893

increasingly worried about what kind of a future they could create for this and maybe other children in a country they considered as lacking in all that made life worth living. It was a heathen country to them. Barbarians were the inhabitants and they were devoid of culture. There was no fine music, no class and no universities to which they had become accustomed. They considered their life well below what standards they had anticipated they might be. It was their concern for the future of their children that caused them to save as much money as they possibly could, always looking toward the day when they could return to their homeland. Rose's pregnancy with her third child, Lena, (the second, a son who died at the age of three) brought it to a head. Their return to Galicia where Rose's parents lived had to be in time for this child to be born "back home." Finally, when enough money had been saved for their passage home, they returned to Galicia, settling in the small village of Brezany, home of Rose's parents. Lena was born there at the home of her grandparents. Once able to travel again safely, Osias and Rose took Jetty and their newborn daughter, Lena, and moved back to Vienna.

Rose, Elsie, Regie, Osias, Jetty and Lena 1903

Osias opened a store where he sold clothing fabrics and similar goods. He became a reasonably financially comfortable merchant. Rose died when my mother was only 16. She had suffered severe headaches, so excruciating that the pain would cause her to scream aloud. She was taken to the hospital and her death occurred within a few days. Today, we believe that she must have had a brain tumor or perhaps an aneurysm. The brain tumor theory most likely is more believable. She died at age 46 in 1910. The weeks to come would indeed bring many difficulties and unforeseen problems. The family not only mourned, but panicked.

It fell upon my mother and her older sister, Jetty, to help with the upbringing of their other sisters. Elsie was the youngest and seven years younger than my mother. Regie was only a couple of years younger than my mother; Jetty was the oldest. The girls stayed at home until they married. Jetty was the first to marry. She was soon followed by my mother who moved to Magdeburg with her new husband in 1922.

Life in Magdeburg was pleasant for my mother and father. The three children to whom mother had given birth were healthy and happy kids. I recall the Sundays spent walking around the park called the Adolph Mittag See, a park located in the heart of Magdeburg. Today, this park is known as the "Kultur Park." All appeared ideal except for the terrible inflation that had set in on Germany after the war and throughout the 1920's. This, of course, resulted from the very difficult armistice conditions dictated at Versailles after the war.

Mark and Lena, having led a loving and generally happy life in Magdeburg, knew little of birth control. When Kurt was less than a year old, my mother announced to Mark that she had once again become pregnant and was in her second month. The news of this event panicked both my mother and father since they felt that a family of three children was surely enough and a full house. The dilemma to follow was a severe trauma to them both as a decision had to be made as to whether or not an abortion needed to be sought or whether a fourth child was to be born. Discussions took

Lena and Mark in the Hartz Mountains 1922

Mark and Lena's Engagement Picture 1922

place daily for some time and although the danger was great, it was decided that an abortion was indeed in store. The decision was extremely difficult in view of the fact that in 1927 abortions were not safe and the loss of life during such surgery was not an uncommon event. With three very, very young children in tow, the possibility of not surviving an abortion was made even graver than might be under different circumstances. There was panic at times, however, when the decision was made it was final and in December 1927 Lena was under the doctor's knife and the embryo was taken from her womb. There was a great relief and after a very short recuperative period, life went on normally as before.

As previously stated, birth control was much of a mystery to Mark and Lena. Though they practiced rhythm and thought that they were being safe, somehow mother's fertility was a momentous problem to them. In 1928 the same situation occurred as mother became aware of another pregnancy. There was little difference in the many hours of discussion which took place then, as compared to what

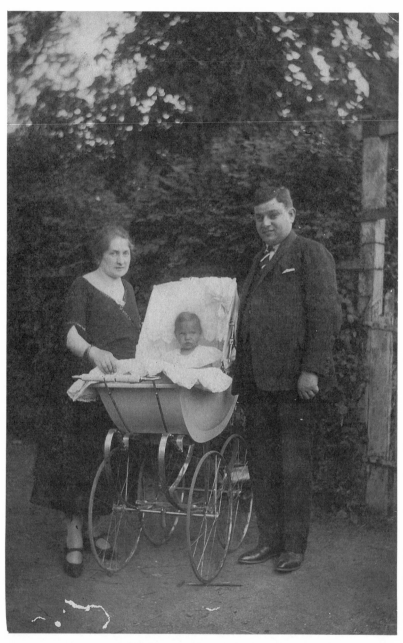

Mark, Lena and Benno 1922

what happened a year previous. Both Mark and Lena were convinced that a fourth child was not to be brought into the world under any circumstances and that once again an abortion was in order. Again, Lena went back to the same doctor who had previously aborted her and a second abortion was performed by him. The second abortion was not quite so successful as the first as an infection set in and mother was ill for some time. It was, indeed, a life threatening situation which, in today's world with such drugs as penicillin, would not have been a problem. The infection took some time to abate and after about two months, mother was well on her way to complete recovery and good health.

The two abortions in two years were a frightening part of my parents' lives which caused them some degree of grief and fear for some time to come. It was decided by both of them, that at no time should any of the three children be made aware of these happenings. The abortions were kept in complete secret for the next approximately 54 years. It was not until 1982, the year after Mark's demise and the year prior to my mother's death, that she sat down with me and Marilyn, my wife, conferring at great length about the ordeals of the abortions which were kept secret for so many, many years. My sister, Renee, and my brother, Benno, were not confided in and to the best of my knowledge, to this day as I write this paragraph, they are unaware of the happenings of 1927 and 1928 with regard to my mother's problems.

It may be concluded that these were life saving decisions on both my parents' part regarding these events. As we look back today, it is to be wondered whether Mark, Lena and their three children would have survived the Holocaust had the abortions not taken place. The burden of years to come when Mark and Lena took their three children to Holland and then to America, might indeed have been too much, had there been five small children rather than three. It may almost be safely assumed that the odyssey to come would likely not have happened with seven rather than five. The choices were good and we should all be grateful that the decisions were made as they were. Were it not for this action, it is likely that this book would never have been written and that the family likely would have met the same fate as Mark's brothers' families in the Ukraine and millions of others. Fate had spared us all.

Benno and Renee 1925

CHAPTER 7

THE RISE OF ADOLPH HITLER

Adolph Hitler was born in Braunau, Austria, and moved to Linz when he was eight years old. He developed tuberculosis at age 16 while he supported himself by painting postcards. His hero and mentor was a fiend named Jorge Lanz Von Liebenfels. Von Liebenfels published papers in the early 1900's about a race of blonde blue-eyed Aryans being superior human beings. He was greatly admired by Hitler for his anti-Semitism and racial views. In actuality he was the first one who turned Hitler on toward his severe anti-Semitism. Adolph Hitler was wounded in the Ardennes in 1916 and spent much time in the hospital pondering the "Jewish problem" as he was recovering from eye wounds suffered when he was gassed by the British. One of

Hitler's life's missions was to annex Austria, then more commonly known as "Ostland" and deal with the Jews there as he envisioned dealing with them in Germany.

In the late 1920's there was almost total anarchy in Germany as the many small factions fought with each other for leadership. The Social Democrats were the strongest group. They were closely followed by the Communists and a party called the National Socialist German Worker's Party, later to be known as the "Nazi" party, which had become very zealous. The German World War I hero, General Erich von Luddendorff, and Ernst Roehm were affiliated with this Workers' Party. They raised considerable amounts of money to finance the movement. Also affiliated with the movement was Julius Streicher, a professional Jew-hater and pornographer who sold pornographic literature nationally. Another Jew-baiter was one Alfred Rosenberg, who played a big part in the German Workers Movement in the 1920's and 1930's as an anti-Semitic hate monger, publishing anti-Jewish literature and rabble rousing his feelings in many speeches.

On September 26, 1923 Chancellor Gustav Stresemann of Germany announced the end of passive acceptance of the French occupation of the Ruhr. In the outcry that followed, separatist movements sprang up in several German states. Bavaria, with its capital in Munich, declared a state of emergency. Dictatorial powers were given to Gustav von Kahr, a Nationalist former Premier. President Friederich Ebert of the German Republic proclaimed a national emergency giving full power to Otto Gessler, Minister of Defense, and General Heinz von Seekt, the Army Commander. The General warned Munich that any uprising would be met with force.

The fiery Hitler saw an opportunity. He did not have the strength to challenge the central government alone and needed help from the Bavarians who were showing caution. Indeed, Ebert's emergency measures seemed to be aimed at Hitler and his ally, General Erich von Luddendorff, the great hero of the war. The Hitler movement wanted to take over Munich and a part of Bavaria and on November 9, 1923 a putsch occurred in a

Munich beer garden. (Putsch refers to the attempted takeover by the German Workers Party.) Hitler learned that Gustav von Kahr, the nationalistic former premier, would address a rally in the beer garden and that other Bavarian leaders would attend. He decided to kidnap them. While von Kahr was speaking, several hundred storm troopers surrounded the hall. Hitler entered, posting a machine gun crew at the door. Climbing up on a table, Hitler fired a shot from his pistol into the ceiling. He got instant attention and he used it to proclaim, "the national revolution has begun."

Hitler took von Kahr's place as the speaker and then forced the Bavarian leader into a private room. With gun in hand, he tried to persuade the gathered assembly to turn the Bavarian dictatorship into a national one and to march on Berlin. Luddendorff appeared and advised the Bavarians to go along with Hitler and create a new "Freies Deutschland" (Free Germany) unencumbered by the much hated and despised Versailles Treaty.

After hearing the Hitler harangue, the

crowd dispersed without acting. Gustav von Kahr and his comrades also dispersed. No plans had been made, no action taken except that Ernst Roehm and some troopers had taken the Munich Army headquarters later that night.

The next morning after the fiasco of the beer garden putsch, Hitler and Luddendorff led a column of storm troopers toward Army headquarters to join Roehm. They approached through a narrow street blocked at the end by police. Someone opened fire. Sixteen police and Nazis lay dead or dying. Many more were hurt and the crowd scattered, including Hitler. Luddendorff stood his ground, erect and unflinching. He was arrested. Hitler was found about 40 miles from Munich in a villa belonging to Ernst Putzi Hanfstaengl, a Harvard graduate and former New York art dealer, who was now a supporter of Hitler's Nazi party. Hitler was not injured except for a grazed shoulder, apparently obtained as he hit the ground when the shooting began. On November 12, Adolph Hitler, the National Socialist German Workers Party Leader, once again tried to whip up a coup against the German National Government. He failed and was put under arrest. Von Kahr moved the Bavarian government to Regensberg, leaving behind posters stating that "Any deals thought to be made with Hitler were extorted at gunpoint and were not to be recognized."

CHAPTER 8

THE EARLY 1920's

Germany attempted to make the repayments demanded by the Versailles Treaty by inflating their currency, which was almost worthless. The period was marked by a tremendous amount of anarchy and numerous political parties vying to be the leader of the country. The largest of these parties was the Social Democrats to which my father belonged. He was, in fact, rather active politically.

On November 15, 1923, this article appeared in a paper:

"German children are making building blocks from bundles of German marks." The value of the currency dropped so quickly and dramatically that machines no longer printed the value of postage stamps. Postal workers did it by hand. At latest count, the American dollar would buy you four trillion marks."

Before the war, the dollar was worth about four marks. In November of 1923, when this article was written, a pound of sugar cost 250 billion marks, a pound of meat more than three trillion, a construction worker in Berlin was paid nearly three trillion marks per day. The fall of the currency was a nightmare for everyone in Germany. The central bank tried to wake the country up from its bad dream but it officially released a new mark worth a trillion of the devalued one. The dollar will buy four of the new marks. All of this was bound to confuse everyone even more because there were now three different currencies circulating in Germany - the new mark, the old mark, and even older gold mark. Most of the smart money had already left the country.

Inflation had gotten so bad that as we look back today it seems without reason and almost impossible to comprehend. It is hard to conceive as I write today, that money was totally and absolutely worthless. Everyone's savings had been totally wiped out. Inflation grew, not by the year, not by the month, or the week or the day and could almost have been seen rising by the hour. Shown here is a clear depiction of the German Mark. It appeared to be nothing but toy money.

Exchange Rates of Dollars and Marks

January	1919	8,9
July	1919	14,0
January	1920	64,8
July	1920	39,5
January	1921	64,9
July	1921	76,7
January	1922	191,8
July	1922	493,2
January	1923	17 972,0
July	1923	353 412,0
August	1923	4 620 455,0
September	1923	98 860 000,0
October	1923	25 260 208 000,0
November	1923	4 200 000 000 000,0

THE EARLY 1920's

In the middle of 1924, Adolph Hitler stood trial for the fiasco of 1923 and was sentenced to five years in prison for the abortive putsch in the beer hall in November of 1923. Lenient judges indicated that Hitler would be eligible for parole in six months. Most of the 60 journalists who covered the trial agreed that the sentence was a mere slap on the wrist. Their stories also transformed Hitler into a national hero and put his name on the front pages in papers all over the world.

Hitler was protected by the Bavarian Minister of Justice during the trial, and the judges allowed him to interrupt frequently and cross-examine witnesses at will. Hitler invoked the name of Richard Wagner as he portrayed himself to be the spirit of German Nationalism and the enemy of Marxism. He vowed that prison would not destroy his will. "You may pronounce us guilty a thousand times but the goddess of the eternal court of history will tear to tatters the brief of the state prosecutor and the sentence of this court."

It was right at this time that Hitler's future ally, Benito Mussolini, received a ringing endorsement at the Italian polls, surprising even his own fascist party as he pulled 64% of the popular vote in a record turnout.

On December 20, 1924, after serving eight months for trying to topple the government in the beer hall coup, Hitler was paroled. The original sentence was five years, and, at the time this was considered very lenient. One must remember that he was convicted of high treason. He was treated royally by the guards at the fortress at Launsberg where he was kept. He was given his own room, a magnificent room at that, overlooking the River Lech. Visitors were allowed to come with gifts and at will. Rudolph Hess voluntarily went to prison to be with Hitler where Hitler spent much of his time dictating a book to his old friend and colleague. This book was to be titled "Mein Kampf" ("My Battle"). The book circulated throughout Germany and told the German people what Hitler would do if he ever came to power.

Since Mark was a bit of a capitalist, he

had strong feelings against the communists and the National Socialist German Worker's Party whose members consisted of mainly bullies and a bunch of anti-Semetic hoodlums. Today they might be compared to the Hell's Angels and the like. There were many motorcycle gangs as part of the Nazi Party, and beatings given to the opposition were commonplace. Other political parties feared very much being in contact with this group which showed their political differences through a great amount of violence. The party was strongest in Munich.

Mark lived in Magdeburg, many miles east of Munich, which was the stronghold of this National Socialist German Worker's Party. He had become quite educated as to the political goings-on and became an activist in the Social Democrat Party. As time went on, the National Socialist German Worker's Party, now renamed the Nazi movement, spread throughout the country, much to Mark's distress.

Friederich Ebert of the Weimar Republic became President of Germany after World War I in 1920. When he died in 1925,

Germany suffered from the fact that there was no real leader. The big wartime heroes in Germany were the Generals Erich von Luddendorff and Paul von Hindenburg who were revered throughout the country for their feats during the war and for their reluctance to give in to the Armistice to which others had agreed. When an election was held Paul von Hindenburg was elected the new President of Germany. He was an old man by this time, feeble and indeed a very poor leader. His popularity, nevertheless, did not wane, and the people looked to him to lead them out of the horrible inflationary cycle that had beset Germany and to bring them back to some kind of prosperity that they had not known since the war. Their hopes and faith were wrongly placed. "Der Alte" (the old one) lived on only in memories, acted on impulse and though loved by the people as a great military leader, knew little or nothing of government. The Weimar Republic under Ebert and Hindenburg gave the country a sad, lame, weak and ineffectual scent. It did much to create an atmosphere of anarchy which threatened Germany most severely. With the lay of the land being what it was, Hitler's operating arena was offered little organized opposition to the very radical reform the Nazi party had in mind. The turf was ripe indeed for anarchy and total political disruption.

CHAPTER 9

THE VILE BEGINNINGS

In February of 1925, my father was doing a wonderful business at the leather goods store. My brother, Benno, born in 1923, was two years old and my sister was one year old. Hitler had been out of prison for only a few months and he wasted little time in reorganizing the political party that was banned after the failed putsch at the Burgerbrau Keller.

Hitler chose another beer hall, The Hoffbrau Haus, to announce the resurgence of the National Socialist German Workers Party, the forerunner of the Nazi Party. His military ally, General Luddendorff, was notably absent, but Hitler was surrounded by other colleagues who believed in his Nazi cause, including

Julius Schaub, Julius Streicher, and Hermann Esser.

Hitler announced a new beginning in the Party newspaper he was printing. He renounced the use of force and pledged to gain power through legal means. This was a new direction as the Nazi Party had previously been a rowdy gang of hoodlums and nothing more.

During his trial, Hitler had impressed many people with his impassioned, nationalistic statements. Most of the country, however, had forgotten him while he was in prison. Fervent followers, however, expected Hitler to make good on the promises he made at the trial, which was really his jumping off point into the political arena. In 1925 he said, "The army we have formed is growing from day to day. I nourish the proud hope that one day the hour will come when these rough companies will grow to battalions, the battalions to regiments, the regiments to divisions, and that the old flags will fly again." Later on that year, Field Marshal Paul von Hindenburg was the victor in an extremely close German presidential election. He beat his principal opponent, Dr. Wilhelm Marx, the Republic Coalition candidate supported by the old Weimar Constitution, the Centrists, the Socialists, and Democrats. The outcome of the close race could not be determined until returns from 33 out of the 35 districts were tabulated. Actually, Hindenburg's victory was attributed to a very strong turnout by the women voters.

The book that Hitler dictated to Rudolph Hess while in jail was published on July 18, 1925. It was an appeal to the German people, a manual for Hitler's growing National Socialist party, and a personal testament. Hitler called for a national revival, a battle against communism, and most of all, the Jews. He expressed his faith in German solidarity. He dedicated the book to his followers who died in the streets of Munich after the abortive putsch.

On August 26, 1926 I was born to Mark and Lena, the same week that Rudolph Valentino died and three weeks after Gertrude Ederly swam the English Channel. Thousands of women were sobbing next to their radios overcome by the news that Rudolph Valentino had passed on. The actor had thrilled them for the past five years with films like "Blood and Sand," "The Young Rajah," and "Cobra." Rudolph Valentino was only 31 years old when he died. A ruptured appendix and gastric ulcer hastened him to a Manhattan hospital. There he spoke his final words, a sad, delirious babble of French and Italian. Pola Negri, the great actress, ordered 4,000 roses for his bier and one fan chose to shoot herself, distraught over Valentino's death.

My father's business was thriving. It totally countered the world wide depression now beginning. On October 24, 1929, America saw Black Thursday, as the stock market crashed. This day began the start of the Depression that lasted for eight to ten years. Losses were in the billions of dollars, although it is difficult to quantify them. Thousands of accounts were wiped out as a record number of shares were traded. It would not be an exaggeration to say that some stocks were almost given away. Nearly 13 million shares were traded and for 1929, that was an unheard of amount. This precipitous decline occurred between 11:15 a.m. and 12 p.m. General Electric dropped 17 points after tumbling 20 points the day before. John Manville lost 25% of its value, as Montgomery Ward fell from 84 to 50 in an hour and one half. No one had ever seen a day like that as the ticker fought a losing battle all day. By the time the final bell sounded at 3 p.m., trading was four hours behind.

On September 14, 1930, the German government suffered a stunning setback in legislative elections and the party that expressed nothing but contempt for the Parliament had registered spectacular gains. Adolph Hitler's national socialists had gone from 12 seats in the old Reichstag to 107 in the new. The Nazis were now more powerful than the communists for the first time and became the second largest party in Germany. Apparently, the hoodlums had arrived.

In 1932, for the runoff election for the Presidency of Germany, the incumbent, Paul von Hindenburg, beat Adolph Hitler by six million votes, yet Hitler had now become a major power. Hindenburg improved upon his showing in the last election, but Hitler did even better, gaining an additional two million votes. Hindenburg received 53% of the vote and Hitler nearly 37%. Traditionalists in Germany had hoped that results would catalyze liberal forces, but Hitler called the race a victory for national Socialism. He said, "Victory obliges me to thank all who worked to create a basis for this victory but carries a heavy obligation to continue. The National Socialists know not what rest is and must not tarry until the goal of German liberation has been reached." These statements were made on April 10, 1932. The rest of Western Europe was greatly alarmed by Adolph Hitler's success. He had been viewed as a warmonger who said that Germany must rise from her ashes and get even for the last war. Hitler's younger followers were fascinated by his fiery oratory. Older Germans were attracted to his hatred of the Jews, war reparations, and the Parliamentary form of government. This was really the first big leap for Adolph Hitler.

There were Nazi party meetings in Mark's apartments. My father's numerous battles with tenants in his buildings, regarding

106

these gatherings became more difficult, and he saw his own wishes for a non-anti-Semitic Germany fading. In previous months when Nazi party meetings were held in his apartments, Mark had gone in violently to break these up. Things were now to be more difficult.

The German Army was weak. Hitler now formed the Sturm Abteilung (S.A.) which was his own private army under his friend Ernst Roehm. Roehm was Chief of Staff of the S.A. In 1934, Hitler began to fear Roehm since he controlled the S.A. with an iron fist. He felt Roehm had gotten too powerful and presented a threat to him, foreseeing him as a rival. With these thoughts in mind, he created the "Schutz Staffel" (S.S.), which means protectorate, to protect himself from his own army that was being ruled by Roehm. This elite group also grew into an army after beginning as a semi-military unit. The S.S. was in reality a large group of bodyguards. It was still a small organization compared to the S.A. Rivalry began and it was soon all too obvious to Hitler that his long-time friend, Ernst Roehm, had to be dispatched and that he would have to take full control of the S.A.

In a rare coincidence fitting Hitler's plans, Roehm was caught in a compromising position with a top aide in the bedroom of his country house. Hitler felt he now had his chance, with good reasons, to do him in. Roehm was given a chance to commit suicide to atone for his indiscretions. When he refused, he was summarily executed. Julius Streicher, his right hand man, was also killed. Hitler stated that the S.A. was threatening to take action against him with the help of an unnamed third power. He hinted at Russia. Whatever the threat, Hitler was once again consolidating power. The event of the killings of Roehm and Streicher became known as the "Night of the Long Knives." The S.A. was totally disarmed by Heinrich Himmler's S.S. which had also taken control of Germany's newly created concentration camps and began assuming the responsibilities that were once held by the S.A. This change reflected Hitler's increasing faith in Himmler and his increasing distrust of the S.A., for all intent and purposes destroyed at the "Night of the Long Knives" the previous month. Hitler had initially felt that the S. A., or Storm Troopers, were indispensable in the Nazi Militia.

As this was happening, Heinrich Himmler gained in status. He had been with Hitler at the beer hall putsch in 1923 and was in control of the S.S. since 1929. He was proud to be a racist; Himmler considered himself a personal friend of Hitler, on the other hand however, so did Roehm until the month before. The S.S. under Himmler was well suited for its new responsibilities. The black shirted defense echelon, the S.S., was an elite corps with unwavering allegiance to the Nazi party. The S.S. kept secrets well, practicing at a half dozen concentration camps found outside Munich and Berlin. Jews, communists and other "enemies of the state" had been sent there by Nazi regimes for quite some time.

My father began to make his plans to leave Magdeburg and go to Holland. This is when my mother and father began their little battles that eventually grew quite large. My mother refused to move. My father won out eventually and we did, in fact, go to Holland. On July 31, 1932, the National Socialists doubled their strength in the legislative elections, claiming to be the biggest party in the Reichstag. The Nazis increased their seats from 107 in 1930 to 229 in 1932. The German Legislature was now very badly divided.

In the election of 1932, Hitler's National Socialist German Workers Party received over one-third of the votes and von Hindenburg's Center Party received slightly over half of the votes. The Communist Party came in third with 10% and Franz von Papen was made Chancellor succeeding Gregar Strasser. In 1933 over three million people were unemployed. On June 30 that year, Hitler replaced what he considered a very inept von Papen and made terror legal. He was, by that time, the Fuhrer and Chancellor, though not officially the head of government.

Paul von Hindenburg as a Social Democrat, had ruled very weakly. When Hitler replaced him, von Papen became a puppet for the regime. On the 30th day of January 1933, one month after secret negotiations, Adolph Hitler had become the

Chancellor of Germany. He took the job over at a very volatile moment in German history. The country was poised on the brink of civil war and anarchy. Almost daily, bloody street battles erupted between Hitler's national socialists and their hated adversaries, the Communists. There was belief that Hitler's thirst for power would be checked by the coalition and the cabinet largely assembled by the deft political skills of the former Chancellor, Franz von Papen. Hitler showed little respect in his first proclamation, however and internal peace was nowhere to be found. He advanced with his shock troops and placed himself at the head of the government to "lead the German people to liberty," he stated. In Berlin, large crowds greeted Hitler's storm troopers as they marched in torchlight parades through the Brandenberg gate. The crowds raised their hands in the Fascist salute to President von Hindenburg who stood in one lighted window of the chancellery, in another stood Adolph Hitler next to his new aviation minister, Hermann Goering.

Hitler, Hermann Goering (the war time aviation hero), and Dr. Wilhelm Fricke were the only Nazis in the cabinet at that time. It had been put together by the former Chancellor, Franz von Papen, after President Hindenburg gave Hitler and the National Party leadership under Alfred Hugenberg an ultimatum and ordered the two adversaries to form a coalition. At that moment, von Papen acted quickly and drew up the cabinet with Hitler as Chancellor, himself as Vice Chancellor, and Alfred Hugenberg as the Minister of Economy and Food.

Two Hitler allies played a key role in the month long secret meetings that brought the Nazi leader to power. They were Cologne banker, Kurt von Schroeder, who had impressed Hitler with his anti-communist rhetoric and Joachim von Ribbentrop, later to become foreign minister. A new era seemed at hand as power plays and back door politics eroded the former status quo. Great changes were in the wind and though direction was still unclear, hardly anyone now doubted that things to come would be different.

CHAPTER 10

THE INNOVATIVE THIRTIES

In 1926 Kurt was born in Magdeburg. In Munich, Hermann Goering, Julius Streicher, Rudolph Hess, and Ernst Roehm formed the original Nazi alliance. Ernst Tahlman was the great communist leader of Germany during these years and the chief antagonist of the Nazis.

The apartment buildings on the Lüneburger Strasse had been our home for a few years. There were approximately 60 apartment units and Mark, having lived in one of the buildings for the past several years, had kept very close control. He was aware of who was who, who was what, and who was where,

Kurt in Magdeburg with his Easter Basket 1931

at most times. He was aware of the political leanings of his tenants. It was in these two buildings that Mark, as an active "Nazi Basher" was both despised and feared by tenants. Many of these Nazis were regulars in the party and had numerous meetings in their apartments to forward their cause. Evictions followed most such meetings and Mark became a marked man. The natural forerunner of things to come was now becoming obvious. It could easily be said, as I look back today, that, indeed, his life was in grave danger and none of us would have survived had we stayed in Magdeburg much longer.

These were wild times throughout the world when the Zeppelin, Germany's dirigible, completed a historic trip around the world. Charles A. Lindbergh had flown across the ocean, and we had seen Black Thursday in the United States when the stock market crashed. Frightened investors ordered their brokers to sell their stocks at whatever price as all stocks plummeted. It was said that walking down Wall Street in those days was dangerous (due to the falling stock brokers). The world was in more or less of a turmoil with events that we look back on today as almost changing the manner in which the earth revolved around on its axis. The 1930's saw the day when New York City installed traffic lights for the first time. Sonia Henie, the nimble Norwegian sprite, captured the affection of figure-skating fans everywhere, having been crowned the World's Amateur Singles Champion for the fourth consecutive time. Greta Garbo was asking for "Whiskey baby and don't be stingy," and Communists battled the police in New York. Former President William Howard Taft died at his home in Washington at age 72, and internal rivalries exploded in China that tested the will and power of Chiang Kai-shek. In America, the nation came to grips with a crime wave as new Chicago gang wars were launched with machine guns. The world of boxing was shocked as Jack Sharkey, in a heavyweight fight, dropped Max Schmelling to the canvas in the fourth round with a very conspicuous low blow, making Max Schmelling the new heavyweight champion of the world.

The 1930's were ushered in with such interesting little asides as Babe Ruth accepting a two-year contract worth $160,000 to play for the New York Yankees. He said he would try to hit a home run for every thousand dollars the club put on the line to get him. In agreeing to the $80,000 a year salary, more than President Herbert Hoover earned, the Babe explained that he had a better year than the President did.

The German government had suffered stunning setbacks in the legislative election. The party that expressed nothing but contempt for Parliament had registered spectacular gains. Adolph Hitler's National Socialist German Worker's Party was becoming the leader in German politics and was controlling the country. The Nazis, as they were now known, were more powerful than their political rivals, taking over everything and everywhere, almost at will. Opposition to their actions melted from fear as the "Nazi" Party steamrolled over all opposition.

The rest of Western Europe was greatly alarmed by the successes of Adolph Hitler. Mark Wallach, of course, was highly distressed at the turn of events. During these trying times, the acute financial crisis closed all banks in Germany. Capital began to flee the country, and the value of the mark continued its decline as Germany was unable to pay its bills.

The Federal Reserve Bank of New York extended some additional help to Germany by announcing it was renewing part of its $100 million credit line that had come due. Other banks said it was time for an international political solution for the crisis. One suggestion was that the German banks not pay out any more marks unless they were traded for foreign exchange.

On August 2, 1934, Paul von Hindenburg died. Hitler finally took over the government officially as President and Chancellor. As a powerful orator, Hitler moved in and convinced the German people that he would finally turn around the disasters that frequented Germany. He would give everyone a job and bring back the prosperity that Germany had not seen for many years. His biggest promise to the German people was that he would correct the errors of the Versailles Treaty signed in

1918. The treaty was hard on the masses and had almost all to do with the major problems at the time.

On the night of February 28, 1933, a mysterious fire destroyed the Reichstag, the German house of government. The chamber where the legislature met had been reduced to rubble and ashes. It was gutted. It was first noticed by a police officer at 9 p.m. that the Reichstag was burning. Before setting the alarm, the officer fired several shots at young men seen running from the scene. The officer seized one young man, a suspect said to be a Communist and identified as Marinus von Derleeuve. The fire would only benefit the Nazi party. The arsonists were undoubtedly the S.A. or the S.S., but the Dutchman was charged.

Hitler's opponents questioned his accusations that Communists were responsible for the Reichstag fire. They wondered what the Communists could have hoped to gain. They also asked why the 24 year old Dutchman accused of the arson would have allowed himself to be captured with all his identification and his Communist party card. The new crackdown on Communists was an outgrowth of the government's repression that had been on the rise since Hitler became Chancellor, shortly before the fire. Three days after Hitler took power, he ordered homes of the Communists searched without warrants. All their meetings had either been banned or strictly controlled. Before the fire, scores of Communists disappeared underground because of the increasing harassment. Communists were not the only targets. Catholics had been attacked by Nazis also. Two dozen provincial governors and police chiefs were dismissed by Goering and replaced by National Socialists. Much of the German population was in a state of panic as the elections approached. Hitler apparently had hoped they would turn to his Nazi party and the program of National Socialism as their only possible hope of salvation during these times of semi-chaos. They had arrested so many political opponents that the jails were bursting.

By the time the firefighters at the Reichstag arrived, the blaze had already spread in many directions. Whoever started the fire apparently set a match to the furniture piled on rugs. The wood paneling, chairs, and desks in the Reichstag chamber were all very dry and they burned easily. The flames crawled to the very top of the elegant Italian Renaissance chamber and caused the ornate glass ceiling to crash to the floor.

10,000 Berliners heard the fire alarm and rushed to police barricades around the burning Reichstag. In the crowd was Hitler, Goering, and Vice Chancellor von Papen. The brave firefighters stopped the fire before it burned through the cupola in the roof. They also saved the library and reading room, where countless priceless documents were stored. The government of Adolph Hitler wasted no time in linking the fire to a Communist conspiracy. He said, "Now you can see what Germany and Europe have to look for from Communism." All this was not true.

Hitler placed Goering in charge of the fire's investigation and before dawn, people were rounding up Communists and locking them up until the investigation had been completed. The Associated Press in the United

States reported that Minister Hermann Goering used the fire as a pretext to place all Communist members of the Reichstag under arrest. Politicians under arrest would not be able to campaign under legislative elections that were less than a week away. That night, President von Hindenburg signed an emergency decree that suspended constitutional guarantees of individual freedom, freedom of the press, private property, and secrecy of postal communication. Communist newspapers were shut down until the election and suspected Communist meeting places were closed. Parts of Berlin began to look more like a police state. The regular police, backed up by Nazi auxiliaries armed with rifles, patrolled through many neighborhoods in armored cars.

In March of 1933, 15,000 people alone were arrested in Prussia. There was nowhere to put them until Heinrich Himmler, the Nazi police commissioner in Munich, came up with a solution. Not more than three weeks after the fire, the Nazis opened their first concentration camp. The first one that was built was at an old powder factory near the town of Dachau, about 10 miles outside of Munich. Three more camps were ready to open near Berlin. It was believed that mostly Communists would be sent to these camps, but they would not be alone. Nazi forces were also arresting Social Democrats, their military units, and Jews.

The following week, Adolph Hitler won what most observers suspected at the time that he wanted from the very beginning. He was granted virtually dictatorial powers, and the German Parliament adjourned for good. The last action by the Reichstag actually gave the supreme powers to Hitler's Cabinet rather than the Nazi leader himself. The President of Germany retained the right to dismiss the Chancellor but almost everyone conceded that President Paul von Hindenburg, an aging figurehead and not much more, was not that able and he had now virtually retired from politics. No one would dare to say aloud that the Cabinet was more powerful than Hitler himself. Hitler had, in fact, taken over, totally, completely and without viable opposition of any kind.

Hitler and his Cabinet could make laws by decree without submitting them to the Reichstag. They had the power to override the Constitution. In his speech to the Parliament before it adjourned, Hitler said the Cabinet is not ready to discuss a return to the monarchy. It was agreed, however, that Hitler was the most powerful Chancellor in history. He wore his Nazi uniform at the podium, but his addresses were restrained. He did use curious expressions, saying at one point, "Treason toward the nation and the Fuhrer shall in the future be stamped out with ruthless barbarity." Later, Minister Goering rebuked the Western press for accusing the government of barbarity. He denied reports that scores of bodies were floating in a Berlin canal and that the Nazis had cut off the ears of some Communists. Shortly thereafter, billboards were put up throughout Germany and a boycott against the Jews became effective. "Jews the World Over Are Trying to Crush New Germany" the signs read. "German People Defend Yourselves - Don't Buy From Jews." Signs such as these were placed throughout the country.

Hitler's government tried to distance

itself from the boycott of Jews and their businesses. Official explanation was that the action was the idea of Nazi citizens. That deception vanished quickly when one of Adolf Hitler's ministers, Dr. Paul Joseph Goebbels, gave a fiercely anti-Semitic speech and explained to an excited audience how the boycott would work. Goebbels claimed that the boycott was temporary but the minister of popular enlightenment and propaganda also threatened to continue it unless Jews around the world stopped their boycott of German goods and stopped accusing the German Government of atrocities. There was not one word of truth in these accusations.

Nazi Germany in early 1933 was indeed a horror as bonfires were made throughout the country to burn books of some of the great German authors, such as Hegel, Marx, and Mann. Book burnings were not only a part of the new Nazi crackdown of intellectual scientists, culture and cultural leaders, but mostly against Jews. Among the individuals dismissed from universities for cultural organizations were writers such as Thomas

Mann, Philosopher Paul Tillich and Nobel Prize winners Gustav Hertz and James Franck.

In June of 1933, acting with the efficiency of a guillotine, Adolf Hitler's government outlawed the Social Democrat Party. The move banished from the cabinet the last major opposition to Hitler, it also dissolved the results of the March elections when the Social Democrats were second in power only to the Nazis. Shortly after that election, Hitler had outlawed the Communist Party. The German Nationalist Party was dissolved and Party Leader Alfred Hoovenberg resigned from the cabinet. Hitler was ruthless and called all opposition subversive and inimical. Goebbels had explained that it was democratic fallacy to believe that people wanted to govern themselves; people only asked to be governed decently, he said. In his speech several days after Goebbels' announcement, Hitler threatened to take children away from their parents who opposed him. "We shall rear them as needed for the Father land," he said during a review of storm troopers.

1933 was indeed quite the year in Germany. As July came about the Germans had been hearing from the Nazis about the perfection of the Aryan race. Hitler's government introduced a new program to weed out Germans who are less than perfect; doctors will sterilize them for the glory of the Reich. Under the new law, men and women will be sterilized if they are idiots or schizophrenic, if they suffer from depression, epilepsy or chorea, or if they are physically weak such as deafness and blindness that are serious or hereditary. The law does not specify whether certain races will be sterilized. Germans must consent to sterilization voluntarily, but it also said that minors can be sterilized involuntarily with the consent of their guardians. The new law showed that the Hitler government was committed to its racial ideology and was willing to interfere with nature itself if necessary.

Hitler was looking for the super Aryan race. He was going to take only pure-blood Aryans into the Army. Everyone else belonged to a lower echelon. To provide Germany with future Aryan-type supermen, he created a program called "Lebensborn." This program was geared toward German women, proclaiming it an honor for any German woman to become pregnant by an Aryan soldier. The government set up homes, similar to vacation type hotels, where many young women lived. The soldiers, "pure" Aryans, often the S.S. men, would visit the women and impregnate them to make more German-Aryan children. The Lebensborn hotels were scattered throughout Germany. The program was originally supervised by Julius Streicher and Alfred Rosenberg and continued on successfully growing annually.

Late in August of 1933 the Nazis began to send Jews to concentration camps, as large numbers of them were being sought and arrested without reason. Some had been in prison for supposedly fighting storm troopers, others for insulting the state, some merely for consorting with German girls and one for imitating a Nazi salute. The outlawed Social Democrat Party had reported that 45,000 prisoners were being held in 65 camps. The London Times at the time reported that many prisoners were being held for their political views and were very poorly fed and beaten on an almost daily basis by the Nazis.

Heinrich Himmler's S.S. gave Hitler an account of the results of the reorganization of the concentration camps. The largest of all was Dachau, and along with Saxenhausen, Lichtstenburg (which was a woman's camp), and Buchenwald, they became the four most feared camps in Germany and were operating with extreme efficiency. The Nazi concentration camps were under the administration of the S.S., elite guard. Each camp was exclusively guarded by 1,500 S.S. men. S.S. Colonel Karl Koch was commander of the very large camp at Buchenwald. Most of the inmates were German political prisoners, homosexuals, and Jews. They had a primitive shelter there and minimum food. Those who were sick and starving were forced to work. It wasn't unusual for a prisoner to lose 50% of his weight in a very short period of time. The camps were built in accordance with the criteria of functional unity and capacity. The Nazi regime had been sending Communists, Jews and other "enemies of the state" to the camps since March. Starvation, horror, terror and death hovered over the camps as clouds on a rainy day. Families of the inmate victims knew nothing of their being tortured or their whereabouts. Torture similar to that practiced in the middle ages was a daily routine as was pain, agony and anguish which often preceded death.

CHAPTER 11

WALLACH'S DILEMMA

Prior to the Reichstag's fire and Hitler's total takeover of government, clandestine Nazi Party meetings were held in apartments Mark owned. When he became aware of such meetings about to take place, Mark and his friends (including police at times since the party had been outlawed) made it a habit to invade the meetings and using clubs, fists and other paraphernalia for violence, broke them up. The tenants were notified the following day that they were to be evicted. Little good followed thereafter and it was not too long before Mark spent more time on this and political concerns than his business. The Nazi bashing that Mark had done for the past few years had then been reduced to no avail. The Nazi party took control and Mark's life was in

Renee, Lena, Kurt and Benno

danger because of actions that he had taken in fighting what was then the regime in power.

My older brother, Benno, had been beaten up in school on a regular basis merely for being a Jew. My sister, Renee, had a very uncomfortable first and second grade, I was shunned by the other children in my Kindergarten class, and was often beaten by the teacher. One memory I have is of being instructed to draw a picture of the pot-bellied stove in the classroom and when it was not drawn to his satisfaction the teacher (a strong, imposing man) hit me repeatedly with a tree switch. At age six, as my mother and governess, Hilda, prepared me for school and walked with me down the street it was a daily occurrence to throw up all over myself and as a consequence have to be returned home. This had gone on for several weeks and it was then decided that Kurt was not to attend school since he was obviously not psychologically prepared. Perhaps Mark and Lena had some insight into what was happening at school where the children and teachers hated someone Jewish to the point where it was impossible for a child to have a normal existence. My father

Benno, Lena, Kurt on lap, Mark and Renee
Magdeburg, Germany 1929

said "How long can this continue?" The sheltered life of prosperity that the Wallach family had, ended and the future looked bleak indeed. The anti-Semitism now creeping through Germany made life unbearable for Mark and his family.

Mark Wallach began to see that things for him and his family would not be good in the future. Although by now Mark was a wealthy man, he felt it prudent to leave everything behind and escape from Magdeburg before the Nazis were to get him. This was to become a reality a very short period of time after the Reichstag fire on February 28, 1933. He had a trusted employee, Fritz Bromann, whom he put in charge of the properties and closed the store that had been so good to him. Bromann turned out to be a very good manager who stood Mark in good stead for several years after Mark left Magdeburg, taking care of the apartment buildings.

In early March 1933, only days after the Reichstag fire, Mark took the family, his three children and wife, to the town of Scheveningen in Holland where he had spent so much time during the First World War. Scheveningen was a lovely resort and life was quite good here. Fritz Bromann saw to it that the monies from the apartment buildings were forwarded to Mark and there were no immediate financial problems. Since Bromann was an Episcopalian, he was not in danger of the horrible anti-Semitism that was sweeping the country. No doubt the Nazis came looking for "Wallach the Jew" after he emigrated to Holland. Persecution of many of his friends back in Magdeburg during 1933 to 1935 was commonplace and heard about monthly by our family.

I remember vividly Mark telling me that the Nazis would put his friends in jail because they were Jews. My mother, of course, would argue vehemently with my father that this was impossible - "they don't throw people in jail because of their religion." I remember most specifically these arguments occurring on a regular basis with both sides sticking tenaciously to their view. Mother always argued that there had to be a reason that a certain friend had wound up in jail, while my father insisted with equal fervor that, in fact, the Nazis were incarcerating their friends only because of their religious beliefs. Even Mark's children were not immune from the dangers of anti-Semitism. He said we needed to be alert and aware of the daily happenings in Germany.

Life in Holland was very good. The North Sea was located about three-quarters of a mile to the west of our home, and a magnificent park, called the Bosches, ringed Scheveningen on the east. The Bosches was a very heavily-wooded piece of land consisting of several hundred acres where we played. We lived on Bossche Straat 154 about three blocks from our school. The three and one-half year interlude we spent there were happy times for us. I recall playing either at the strand (beach) or in the Bosches with two friends (Harry Smith and Kurt Berman). The only cloud on the horizon during this happy time was when my sister, Renee, was kidnapped from school and taken to the dunes. Exact details were not disclosed, it was kept very quiet and was not talked about. Overall, it was a wonderful life. There was no anti-Semitism in Holland and we children, although quite foreign to the language, customs and clothing of the Dutch, slowly assimilated into the Dutch lifestyle and lived happily.

There was no work for my father, and, for the first time in his life, he felt totally unproductive. He decided it was time to open his own business. After living in the Hague for six months, Mark visited Amsterdam and rented a store on the Reguliers Bree Straat in downtown Amsterdam, right around the corner from the famed Rijks Museum. My father hired a man who was very knowledgeable about ice cream and between the two of them, they developed recipes for various flavors, previously unknown. Until this time, one could purchase any flavor of ice cream desired, as long as it was chocolate or vanilla. My father and his employee developed the recipes for exotic flavors of ice cream such as strawberry, cherry, mocha, banana, etc., until they had approximately 30 different flavors served in many different ways. It was the first time that any such great variety of flavors was presented to the public. The store opened in late 1933 and became an immediate success. At times, there were lines of people waiting to get into the store to try these newfangled desserts. To say the business thrived would be an understatement.

Mid December 1934, a dreary snow flaked afternoon, the ice cream parlor was half empty with only a few people partaking of the goodies. In a corner booth a couple sat sipping one dish after another and remained in the booth for a period of somewhere between an hour and a half or two. In total, they consumed about eight or ten different dishes and were busily engaged in heavy dialogue. A lengthy stay and most unusual action of having ordered at least four or five different dishes each made Mark wonder what and why. He had never had an experience with customers of this nature. On occasion some one or two people might come in and order two dishes each and stay for a period of a half an hour or forty-five minutes, but eight or ten dishes for the two people over a period of two hours was quite unusual and not understood.

After a little while, my father went over to the table and introduced himself as the owner and asked if he could sit down. He found that the people were Americans and did not speak Dutch. The conversation he had attempted with this couple was quite difficult indeed, but somehow they managed to communicate and stated that they were so very, very pleased and excited about all the various dishes of ice creams that were available. Questions such as, "Where did you ever get these ideas?" and "How long have you been doing this?", etc., etc., came through even though the language barrier was a severe handicap to all parties. There was about as much communication with hands as there was with audible sound. After my dad had introduced himself to the couple, they introduced themselves to him as Mr. and Mrs. Howard Johnson from America. Mr. Johnson had just signed a contract with the state of Pennsylvania for a number of ice cream outlets on the Pennsylvania Turnpike which was then nearing completion. He was indeed interested to see what this store in Amsterdam was offering that created so much interest and caused so many people to flock into it. Mr. Johnson said not only that he enjoyed everything that he had tasted so much, but that he would be back the following day. Cordial greetings were exchanged and the Johnsons left, never to be seen again. It was not more than two years later that similar dishes were to be served on the Pennsylvania Turnpike under the name of Howard Johnson Ice Cream. Although there were no such things as patents on ice cream, in the future all these flavors Mark discovered would, in the next ten years, become favorite dishes all across the United States. For much of the rest of his life, when Mark saw the Howard Johnson stores, he smiled with glee knowing that somehow he was partially responsible for their being.

The name of my father's ice cream store was the "Ijs Paleis Hollandia," translated into the English, it means "Ice Cream Palace of Holland." Once again, Mark had pulled himself up with a new beginning and had created a wonderful moneymaking business. His business acumen was indeed to be admired. All appeared ideal in our lives, however in my father's mind, this was far from the case. Mark Wallach always had a touch of paranoia concerning the Nazi movement. He continued his constant quest for more knowledge of the political situation in

141

Germany. Mark convinced himself that the goings on there could only lead to terrible things for the continent with Jews being arrested and incarcerated by the Nazis and the spreading of ultra-Nationalism in Germany. It should be noted that this was as early as 1933 and much earlier, when Mark felt these rumblings.

It was August 2, 1934 that President Paul Von Hindenburg died. Adolf Hitler had more power than Stalin or Mussolini at this point. A correspondent for the NY TIMES said that he was more powerful than the Genghis Khan. Hitler's critics pointed out that 10% of the voters dared to say no, and 1,000,000 of them expressed their dissatisfaction by tampering with the ballots. Many of these, however, wound up in concentration camps, never to be heard from again.

By 1935, there were still no thoughts at all on most people's minds of anything being wrong in Europe. At that time, Hitler was looked upon as a great leader of the German people, bringing them back from the terrible inflation suffered during the 1920's and bringing a stability to Germany that it had not experienced in years. Jobs were plentiful and prosperity reigned, the country was in wonderful shape. My father saw things differently, however. He had read Hitler's "Mein Kampf" and predicted that eventually, the ultra-Nationalism would lead to persecution of the Jews, a persecution similar to the type the Czar had inflicted upon the Jews in the Ukraine during my father's youth. Mark remembered how anti-Semitism had historically taken place around the world. His feelings were looked upon as being a bit eccentric, not only by my mother but to those whom he expressed his views of pessimism and a grim future for Europe. History was to show that Mark was a true visionary as he was totally correct in his assessment regarding Hitler's reign of terror yet to come.

Mark's love for his immediate family, i.e., Lena and his three children, was true and deep. No father could have been more loving, kind and responsible than he. The high regard and love for family went beyond the immediate four of us. His love for the brothers and their wives and children left behind in eastern

Europe was not much less. Indeed, he was a devoted man to the core and he realized that the possibility was very strong that immigration to the United States would soon have to become a reality. His heart was breaking for the brothers he might not see again. A trip back home was called for. Traveling from Scheveningen to Galicia in 1935 for a last visit was mandated though a difficult task. Yet he felt the trip needed to be made. The distance was great and the railroads left much to be desired. Nevertheless, Mark chose to make a final journey back to Chorostkow and Tarnopol to see his family once again, possibly for the last time. While corresponding with them, they had told him much of their business with regard to the importing from western Poland of hardware supplies, nails, screws, fasteners and even bricks. Bringing these supplies in from distant places was a part of their importing business. Most of the goods were either made, or came directly from the town of Oswiecim, a small city near west central Poland. Brother Moses wrote that since Mark was coming to Chorostkow and Tarnopol and would surely pass, if not stop at Oswiecim, that he should arrange to purchase a rather large order of goods that was needed by the business.

Oswiecim was not only a major distribution center, but was also the site of a large army camp which was used during World War I and had since been more or less abandoned. Some of the barracks, in fact, still in good condition were used as warehouses. Little did the family in Poland, or Mark, realize that Oswiecim and the old army camp were, in reality, soon to be known as Auschwitz, which in the next few years would become the greatest killing camp of all time. Auschwitz (Oswiecim), the infamous home of terror and torture, the place from which Dr. Joseph Mengele did human experiments testing pain tolerances, amputations sans anesthesiology, starvation and murder, was the site from which Mark was to purchase goods. Mark could not have had any idea of what place he was about to visit. Not in his wildest imagination could he, nor anyone else for that matter, ever conjure up thoughts as to the nightmarish abyss to which he would soon go.

Upon arrival in Oswiecim, Mark spent considerable time purchasing goods. The hardware and all other supplies which the family had wanted had to be ordered. It was Mark's duty to see to it that it was shipped so that it would arrive safely in Tarnopol and it was his job to see to it that the importation would go without a hitch and that all goods were received for monies paid. This he did during a three-day stint in this small city.

When all goods were gathered, paid for, and shipped, Mark realized that it would only take two more days for him to arrive in Chorostkow. While at the station, the dilemma came to light that in two days it would be Saturday, the "Sabbath." Under no circumstances would his father have allowed him to travel on the holy day, and thus, Mark remained two more days in Oswiecim so as not to arrive at the home of his family on the Sabbath. The second day of the delay he spent much of his time in the railroad station when he found that there were no rooms to be had and that he would be stranded for 12 hours. By Monday morning, Mark arrived in Chorostkow to the great joy of his brothers, father and family. Upon arrival at the train station in Chorostkow, he saw a big sign which read, WALLACHOVKE. The train station in Chorostkow had been named Wallachovke, no doubt in honor of David Eli. My father's pride, at that moment, could have been felt throughout the Ukraine.

One of the joys of coming home was the many memories that Chorostkow and Tarnopol had for Mark. He recalled that as a teenager wanting to prove his worth, he had brought in a supply of a "special" product which would make animals grow bigger. He had spent considerable time peddling this product to all the farmers in the area and yet, was unable to prove his point that if the herds were fed Mark's miracle food, that the animals would become 15% larger, the meat more choice and the milk better tasting. This product was a miracle elixir, so he had stated as convincingly as he could, over and over again, to all who would listen or could conceivably become a prospective purchaser.

The "elixir" did not sell at all. Now Mark had invented a new plan whereby he enlisted the aid of all his old friends and one of his brothers who would now go around to all of the stores and some farmers who might be interested in this type of a product, asking them if they could get him a supply of it since it was so good. They were so successful in spreading the word about the product in this manner that whatever supply Mark had was immediately sold out. He remembered with humor he had made money with it. However he was unable to get any more and the venture died. This is one of many old remembrances that the family shared during Mark's visit, along with so many others. There was much joy in the homecoming parties, a bit of "schnapps," horseplay, and joy was the order of the day.

Yet, the visit was a sad one. Mark's insistence about Germany's and Europe's plight as it related to his view of Adolph Hitler's ambitions, put fear into the hearts of the family. The disasters of the past via anti-Semitic horrors, were all too well documented and known through first-hand experience. Was Mark accurate in his assessments? Was he merely just a bit paranoid, or were his very pessimistic thoughts for the future actually to become reality? Whatever the case, Mark had made it clear he intended to leave Europe and immigrate to the United States with his family, where it would be safe. He felt so sure of impending calamity that he strongly urged the members of his family to come with him to America and escape the looming disasters he was imagining and which he was sure would soon become reality. After all, he pleaded, Joe and Adolph, the two brothers, were already there. Surely they would help them all to settle in, assimilate and help them to make a new life.

Most of Mark's pleas fell on seemingly deaf ears. "Yes, it would be a great idea." "Yes, there was much to be said for Mark's views," they stated. However, moving families with young children half way around the world to a new culture, strange language and guaranteed uncertainties was asking too much. In the end, and to Mark's distress, the last words were to the negative. Oh, how different things would have been had Mark prevailed.

149

CHAPTER 12

MARK'S VISIT

Kurt's parents were a loving pair, and although Mark adored his family and showed it at all times, it was probably most obvious in his efforts to provide them with a good life for the future through success in business. Mark was jovial and, at times, carefree for the most part, yet feared that he was right in becoming so increasingly worried about the future. News from Magdeburg concerning friends in trouble with the law was a strain on him. At times the jovial fellow was not at all jovial but seemed to be carrying the load of the world on his shoulders. His fears for what was to come became obvious and it was then that Lena finally agreed that there might possibly be something to her husband's fears about Germany, as more of their friends in Magdeburg were being sent off to jail and eventually being sent to a concentration camp known as Buchenwald.

My mother acquiesced to Mark's belief that their Jewish friends in Germany were indeed being singled out and persecuted because of their faith. At this time, approximately mid-1935, Mark became so increasingly worried about the future, that Lena finally agreed that he could go to the United States alone on a three-week vacation to visit his brothers and look things over in the event that the future would take a turn for the worse as he predicted and that we would once again need to flee.

It is important to remember that Lena despised America due to her parents' experiences when they lived in New York. She remembered their stories of the horrid sweatshops and terrible living conditions before her birth. She thought America to be barbaric. However, Lena felt she had no choice but to agree to Mark's trip there for the sake of her family's future.

Nevertheless, it was her hope that Mark would find things too difficult in that far off land as

Mark (seated, second from left) coming to the United States 1935

news of the depression sweeping across America made its way into the Dutch newspapers.

In any event, Mark went to the United States and visited his brother, A.T. (Adolph Tobias) in Cleveland, Ohio. It was the first time he had seen A.T. in many years. Mark also met with his other brother, Joseph, who lived in Detroit, on several occasions. The three weeks that Mark spent in America were none too promising regarding his potential for making a living in that country. It was very important to Mark that he be able to establish himself in business as he had a family to support. Holland's immigration laws disallowed any capital leaving the country in excess of 5,000 guilders. The economic problems were discussed at great length among Mark and his brothers. I would come to the conclusion that although both brothers wanted very much for Mark to come to the United States, they realized that his chances of being able to eke out a living during the height of the depression were minimal.

The three brothers were cut from the

same cloth. To know one was actually to know them all. They had genetic traits that were so similar that, at times, they surprised even themselves. They were kind, loving people, meticulous almost to exaggeration, and to a degree, perfectionists. Their main motivations in life appeared to be the betterment of their families, of whom they each took care, all too well. The kindness and love of their families extended also to one another. Although I have not had the privilege of meeting the other brothers who lived in the Ukraine, I must believe as I write this today, that they were likely not different from A.T., Joe and Mark. All were hell bent on success in business and were honest to a T. Never was a dishonest dollar made and their word was their bond. The common denominator was that all three had been successful almost from the word go.

A.T., as a youngster, fled the Ukraine as the first one to leave the nest. He came to the United States slightly before the year 1900, went directly to Cleveland and began a career in the real estate business. This career lasted until his demise and was

Mark, A.T. and Joe in Cleveland, Ohio 1937

highlighted by numerous successes. After working hard for a number of years, he eventually wound up as a fee simple owner of numerous properties including several in downtown Cleveland. The brothers had a keen sense of humor and never passed up the opportunity to tell a joke, rib a friend or tell a tale. One instance sticks out in my mind as being typical of A.T.'s sense of humor. Adolph was a devout cigar smoker and as he was able to afford them, he smoked 7 inch long cigars, daily. One day, standing on a very busy downtown corner, he met his friend who saw him smoking the cigar and asked, "How much does one of those cigars cost, A.T.?" A.T. glibly stared him in the face and said, "About a dollar." His friend then asked, "How many of those do you smoke a day?" A.T. replied, "Likely seven or eight." After pondering these answers for a moment, his friend asked, "How long have you been smoking these?" and Adolph said, "Probably 20 or 25 years." His friend stood there for a moment and all of a sudden pointed to a building, about 12 stories high which stood across the street, and said, "Adolph, if you didn't smoke those cigars for all those many years, you could probably own that building over there." A.T. stared him in the face and said, "Do you smoke?" His friend said, "No, absolutely not, I do not." A.T. asked, "Do you own that building across the street?" "Nope, I don't," said his friend, at which point A.T. replied, "Well, I do." The writer will only testify to the fact that this is the way Adolph told the story. Whether or not it ever happened, I would leave to someone else's opinion.

Joe was a character all his own. As an example of his psyche, it is interesting to note that when he came to the American shores very early in 1900, he got off the ship almost penniless, went through Ellis Island and was admitted to the United States. One of the first things he did on the second day in this country was to go to a medium size office building in New York where he contacted the building manager and inquired as to whether there were any offices for rent. The manager told him he was in luck since there was an office available. He showed it to Joe who liked it quite well. Half of the few dollars that Joe had in his pocket were given to the manager. The following day a sign painter appeared painting a sign, "S. Joseph Wallach, President" on the front door. (He had no idea of what he would be doing, let alone what it might be of which he was to be president.) This was Joe's beginning in the United States. The camaraderie, comedy, love of family, ambition to succeed, and kindness were traits that the three brothers had in common. To know them was to love them.

Mark returned to Scheveningen after his visit to America, proclaiming there was gold in the streets. He spoke enthusiastically of the wonderful opportunities available in Cleveland and how, under no circumstances, could the family remain in Holland in view of what was happening in Germany. Mark felt certain that Germany's persecution of the Jews would soon spread throughout Europe. "The land of promise and opportunity awaited them in the United States," he said. Of course, this was a lie, and I don't know if my mother saw through this or not. America was in the grips of the worst depression in its history and anyone who could put food on the table and pay the rent was considered highly successful.

Someone who could accomplish these tasks was admired. Times in America were indeed hard. The government-sponsored programs such as the C.C.C. and the W.P.A. fed millions, as did the many soup-kitchens that were prevalent throughout the country. Franklin Delano Roosevelt's New Deal was proving to be successful, yet starvation conditions existed in pockets of the United States. Not only did the U.S. have its major economic problems, but it was still recuperating from the dust storms that had severely damaged the mid-west region of the country. These violent storms ravaged Kansas, Eastern Colorado, Wyoming, Oklahoma, Texas, and parts of New Mexico. Breathing was difficult and dangerous and this part of the country experienced major problems. Near starvation conditions were not uncommon.

In Europe, a White Paper Report signed by Prime Minister Ramsay Macdonald had said that British Defense needed bolstering because of Germany's aggressive spirit and because all over the world, armaments were being increased. In 1935, Germany instituted compulsory conscription of young men into military service, violating the 1918 Versailles Treaty of not allowing Germany to have more than 100,000 troops. This action by Germany had breached all of the Versailles Treaty's Military Clauses. The British concern about Germany heightened when the Third Reich announced that it was re-instituting military conscription. The German press exalted the move with headlines such as "End of Versailles, Germany Free Again." The text of Germany's legislation stated that only through the rebirth of the German Army could the German people be protected from an arms-bristling Europe. Responses were predictably mixed with most of the great powers upset. France was discouraged but not surprised. England was angered and willing to send Foreign Minister John Simon to Berlin for negotiations. Japan was outwardly silent but appeared to be happy with the renewal of Germany's militarism.

Soon, Italy's Benito Mussolini followed suit by expanding Italy's conscription laws to include the class of 1911. In the following month, Italy would have one million men armed and ready to fight. While many

Europeans were uncertain of what Mussolini's motives were, clearly Italy's involvement in Ethiopia did not require such military strength. The dictator told crowds gathered at Fascist celebrations that he wanted the Italian people to know that no event would catch them unprepared. The scenario in Germany, Italy, France, and England did not produce the most optimistic thoughts for the future.

With his new powers, Hitler could make war, peace, create new laws, abolish old ones, execute suspects and pardon convicts. He was legislator and executive in everything which was represented by the law. Nearing the end of 1935 in Nuremberg Hitler unveiled new laws that stated categorically that Jews are not German citizens and therefore could never vote or participate in German politics. The laws on German citizenship, blood and honor, prohibit Jews from marrying German citizens, having extramarital relations with German citizens, employing German women less than 45 years old, raising the German flag, etc. The new law said violators would be sentenced to prison terms. All these stories came back to my father in Holland who was daily fearful of the news that came both via newspaper and letters from his friends back in Magdeburg. Were his theories about future predicted disasters coming into fruition?

While my father was considering the family's move to America, things in Europe were rapidly progressing downhill, just as he had feared. Adolph Hitler was receiving his most enthusiastic ovations and accolades. It had been almost a year since Hitler established obligatory military service in Germany. On March 7, 1936 he put this military might to use as his armies crossed into the Rhineland, which was a demilitarized area under French control as dictated by the Treaty of Versailles. Hitler, in a speech to the Reichstag, called it a "close to the struggle for German equality." He explained that Germany was no longer bound by the treaty because of the mutual assistance pact between France and the Soviet Union. Hitler said he felt he was compelled to move his troops because of the Communist threat and what he called France and Russia's iron ring around the Reich. He was also concerned about overtures France had made to Britain for a defense treaty. British foreign secretary, Anthony Eden, harshly condemned the German move into the Rhineland but neither England nor France showed any signs of taking any military action.

In March of 1936, when Hitler invaded the Rhineland, the part of Germany deeded to France in 1918, France did not object. It must be remembered that the French could have easily defeated Hitler at that time. They were a much more powerful country, but they stood idly by and let the Nazis move in to avoid a war.

In the meantime, in Austria, Engelbert Dolphuss, the Austrian Premier, was Hitler's biggest enemy, opposing the "Anschluss." He spoke vehemently of the dangers of Nazism. Hitler had Dolphuss murdered later in 1936 to end this unwanted opposition.

In Italy, Benito Mussolini's Palazzo Venicia was bathed in bright lights as crowds packed into the square as the Il Duce proclaimed victory in Ethiopia and the rebirth of an empire. The battle in Ethiopia had been going on for some time as the Italians sought to conquer that nation fully. Mussolini stated in his address, "Italy at last has her empire. It is a fascist empire because it bears the indestructible sign of the will and power of Rome." Ethiopia had been formally annexed to Italy, Mussolini said. Victor Emmanuel, the king, also assumed the title of Emperor. Marshal Pietro Badoglio, the victorious general had been named Viceroy. He would administer the new colonial territory in Africa. Marshal Badoglio entered Addis Ababa on May 5, 1936. Part of the capital city had been pillaged and burned after the quick departure of Emperor Halie Salasi. Badoglio was saluted by a long line of Italian soldiers and Ethiopian civilians as he took possession of the city.

In Geneva the League of Nations showed very little signs of listening to sanctions against Italy, despite the end of the war for which the world and long waited. During this period, Mussolini was trying to patch up his relations with Britain and he proclaimed that this victory would put Italy into the league of satisfied colonial powers seeking no more territorial gains for itself.

In mid-1936 the civil war in Spain erupted. In early July General Francisco Franco, leader of the Fascist troops vowed to press on until he installed himself as the Dictator in Madrid. Loyalist forces were under order to fight the rebels to the death and prevent turning Madrid into a tomb of fascism. This outbreak of war unleashed tensions throughout Europe as the Italians and Germans both began to assist Franco in his fight against the Loyalist troops of Spain. The American Government quickly acted to remove Americans trapped in the war and 150 Americans ran for shelter to the Madrid Embassy as the Civil War got hot. Many of them were sleeping on floors and in bathtubs. The American liner Exeter made an unscheduled stop in Barcelona and evacuated 160 Americans. The outbreak of this war unleashed tensions throughout Europe. France sent urgent appeals to Italy and Britain called for a joint conference to emphasize the need for neutrality. In Madrid, the interior minister ordered house to house searches for rebels and arms. Hundreds of rebels were arrested, many never to be seen again. The rebels, with Hitler and Mussolini's aid were too much for the loyalist regime, which soon would fall under the onslaught.

Germany and Japan signed an anti-communist pact, pledging cooperation in defending against the spread of Soviet influence. The treaty that was described as a measure for defense of European culture and civilization and world peace complemented a similar pact reached the previous month between Germany and Italy. In effect, an anticommunist axis had now been forged among the three states and the result was to bring to reality German Chancellor Adolf Hitler's dream of a worldwide anti-communist block. The text of the German/Japanese treaty didn't mention the Soviet Union, rather it stated the objective was a police pact for the mutual cooperation directed against international activity of Moscow communist influence throughout the world. Despite denials from both Berlin and Tokyo, suspicion was voiced in Europe that the anticommunist front was a cover for traditional military alliance and a creation of spheres of influence in the western Pacific and the East Indies.

Highlights in 1937, found Leon Trotsky, the exiled Soviet leader being pushed out of Russia, and living in Mexico. He said that a new revolution was necessary to overthrow Joseph Stalin and his Soviet bureaucracy. He declared that Stalin should be eliminated but not killed. Trotsky objected to the current Soviet bureaucracy and its privileges. He added that if a war came and Russia found itself allied with Britain and France, it might emerge capitalistic because it now teeters between socialism and capitalism and the allies would bring political pressure to bear. If the Soviet Union resists this pressure, her allies would go after her after the war.

It was during these talks that Germany got very active in the war against the loyalist troops of Spain as German bombers devastated Spanish cities. In April of 1937, hundreds of people, mainly civilians were dead in the town of Guernica, Spain near Bilbao. They were killed by German war planes that swept out of the sky to strafe market places and farm houses. The small town was still burning almost a week later.

The civil war that had been going on in Spain was of great interest to Mark due to the fact that the German Luftwaffe was bombing cities in Spain, killing hundreds of people in a war in which Germany had no part. "What reason was there for this?" Junkers and Heinkel bombers dropped dozens of tons of bombs and grenades and fire bombs as well as firing mercilessly at peasants in the fields. Those who were lucky enough to escape were still streaming into cities where they were bombed almost out of existence. Civil war raged and Germany, which was "not involved," rejected any responsibility for these raids. Nevertheless, it was very difficult to hide the fact that these were German bombers with German pilots that had joined the rebellion against the Spanish government. "Was Hitler testing his military forces for the future?" Mark often discussed this German involvement. His reasoning that these were "military exercises" for future battles convinced him more every day of Hitler's sinister intentions.

While Spain was being ravaged, Joseph Stalin's purges reached into the highest levels of the Russian military. At a secret trial, eight generals and Marshals were sentenced to death for treason and were executed. Officials say they all pleaded guilty to charges of trying to overthrow the Stalin regime. "Down with the traitors," Pravda, the official communist party newspaper declared, "No mercy to spies and betrayers." One of the generals executed was Marshal Mikhail Tukhachevsky who, until recently, had been Vice Commissar of Defense. The secret police arrested him in the middle of the night and wounded him when he allegedly tried to escape. The generals were all accused of conspiring against the Soviet Union with an unnamed foreign power, presumably Germany. Pravda criticized what it called, "The Foul Boot of German and Japanese Fascism." "The reptile of fascist espionage has many heads," Pravda said. "But we will cut off every head, paralyze and sever every tentacle and extract the snake's venom."

In May 1937, the German dirigible airship Hindenburg was destroyed by fire in a disaster that killed 35 of its 97 passengers and crew. The giant airship was consumed in minutes as it came in for a landing at the

Naval Air Station in Lakehurst, New Jersey. The news of this was on the radio both day and night and both mother and dad kept their ears glued to newscasts hoping to hear more news of the tragedy which happened as the Hindenburg blew up. The cause of the fire was unknown but was believed to have started when either static electricity or sparks from the engine ignited hydrogen gas that was being released preparatory to landing. Until that disaster, the Hindenburg had a perfect safety record in 10 round trips it made across the Atlantic with over 1,000 passengers. They heard on the news one evening that the Hindenburg was 12 hours late on this flight because of head winds encountered over the Atlantic and it had cruised slowly down the east coast so that it would arrive at dusk, the best time for landing. The airship dropped in two landing lines early in the evening and was settling toward the earth when the hydrogen caught fire. Witnesses heard a boom and saw flashes from the ship's rear gondola. The flames enveloped the airship in moments and the Hindenburg collapsed in clouds of smoke. Many lives were saved by Navy personnel and crew members.

MARK'S VISIT

The tragedy ended an era of dirigibles as no such ship as the Hindenburg was ever again to fly the skies. The soundness of design and the general principle of its construction was found, after much study, to be totally faulty and should never have been built. Indeed, many studies after the disaster showed that the post-tragedy studies should have been conducted prior to the construction of such an airship. The era of the dirigible was over.

Soon after the disaster of the Hindenberg, in Germany the streets of Nuremberg were lined with storm troopers and all the church bells rang at once as Adolph Hitler arrived for the opening of the National Socialist Congress. The event was designed to be the largest display of Nazi power in Germany's history. The size of the congress was staggering. Hitler reviewed a parade of 600,000 men. Hundreds of trains were transporting army and para-military units to Nuremberg. The men were being housed in thirteen separate tent cities.

An anti-bolshevik exhibit that linked communism with Judaism was opened that day.

Local Nazi leaders made the astounding charge that the Talmud gives Jews the right to murder people who are not Jewish.

The diplomatic corps., including the American charge d'affaires, was due in a few days. Benito Mussolini also came for the event. Hitler and Mussolini exchanged high military honors and Hitler greeted Il Duce as an upholder of Fascism and one of Europe's leading anti-communists.

The plight of the Jews in Europe continued pathetically, as many tried to leave the country and found havens to be few and far between. Rejecting previous principles of economic absorptive capacity, the Palestine government had issued an ordinance restricting Jewish immigration. The limits of Jewish immigration would depend, not on economic circumstances, but on national political conditions.

The Hebrew press vehemently attacked the new ordinance. It claimed Britain's wording of the law "Persons of Jewish Faith" clearly violated the mandate which stated, "all religions in Palestine were to stand on an equal basis." Newspapers in Bethlehem and Jerusalem also pointed to the council of the League of Nations, which had demanded that England adhere to the economic absorptive principle.

Since July, Britain, as the mandatory power in this region, proposed a partition of Palestine into Arab and Jewish states, 39 people had died from terrorist attacks due to this. Snipers had fired on police stations near Bethlehem. Exodus to the sought after country of Palestine where so many Jews lived was now severely restricted by the British government.

CHAPTER 13

THE AWAITED JOURNEY

My mother and father had many arguments over the possibility of emigrating to the United States. Mother was adamant in her feelings of not moving her family to America. My father was equally adamant that the family could no longer remain in Europe. While Mark and Lena had this great difference of opinion, Mark became very ill one day in late 1935 with severe pains in his abdomen. The doctor was confused as to his diagnosis, and sent him to the hospital. He underwent an exploratory operation resulting in the removal of his appendix. I am still not quite sure what was wrong with him, and, of course, the decision about moving to the United States was put on the back burner. My father took a long time to recover from his operation, as the doctors had made an incision from the upper-stomach region to the groin area during the surgery. Today, this major surgery would not have been considered. Mark's operation was quite serious and it took him months to recuperate from the trauma of the surgery. Nothing was found. The surgery itself was far more traumatic than any malady which may or may not have existed. A wide and ugly scar from his stomach to his groin of about 12 inches marked him the rest of his life.

Mark recovered and went back to his business at the Ice Palace in Amsterdam. The business continued to thrive and was filled to capacity for 14 hours a day as it had from its inception in 1933. Mark's idea of coming to the United States had not changed. He was hell-bent on taking his family there to protect them from the fiery atmosphere of Europe that he felt would soon explode. He had unbelievable foresight and his fears soon showed they were well founded. Almost to the month and year, his predictions became reality. He continued his tirade against my mother's objections concerning the family's move to the United States. The arguments between them were incessant, a daily occurrence, and quite severe in nature at times. We, as children, were very upset at seeing our parents argue so vehemently with each other.

Soon my father, unbeknownst to my mother, did a considerable amount of traveling throughout Holland. (Since Holland is so small he accomplished this readily.) During his travels throughout the country, he purchased herring and cheese, Holland's main export products at the time. Although he knew nothing concerning these products, he bought countless barrels of herring and cheese that he subsequently warehoused. When Mark learned, in early 1936, that the largest ship in the world was being built in England, he secretly rented a part of the lower commercial deck of this new ship to transport the herring and cheese to the United States. His secret was very well kept. No one had the slightest inkling of his plans; not even Lena suspected. Mark arranged with the Cunard White Star Line, owner of this new vessel, the Queen Mary, to load his cargo once the shipbuilding was completed. Mark almost forcibly took his family to Southampton, England in late

October 1936. He sold almost all our possessions in Scheveningen and boarded the family on the Queen Mary for its semi-maiden voyage to America. My mother resigned herself to this inevitable move and her family began its five-day journey across the Atlantic Ocean to the United States where her husband sought a new life for his family.

This move was the height of bravery, since it was not possible for the family to take money out of Holland. Any immediate livelihood or financial security they would have in the strange country of America had to come from the sale of the herring and cheese loaded on the ship on which the family sailed. When we arrived at the docks in New York, we all looked down as seemingly countless numbers of barrels of herring and cheese were unloaded. We were extremely excited as my father proclaimed, "It's all ours." However, we were also fearful and puzzled at the prospect of our adventures to come in this new country. We had changed our language three and one-half years earlier from German to Dutch and made the adjustments needed to learn the customs and culture of Holland.

Now we were facing the daunting task of having to learn the English language and American customs. This prospect did not scare us children, as we fully understood the undertaking. It was of great concern, however, to my parents.

The family stayed in New York for three days. My father was in the herring and cheese business only briefly. By the end of the third day in New York, he had sold almost all of the barrels of herring and cheese that he had transported from Holland. He was, once again, reasonably financially secure, and the fear of economic failure and the inability to care for his family greatly diminished.

On our fourth day in America, the family boarded a train and traveled to Cleveland, Ohio. Our train journey was exciting and marked by fear and anticipation of the future. We moved in with my uncle, A.T., in Shaker Heights, a suburb of Cleveland. Our family stayed with A.T. and his family for a few weeks. We children attended Landsmere Elementary School, and soon our family moved to a three-bedroom, two-bath apartment

Back row: Benno, Lena, Mark, Margaret
Front row: Kurt, Renee, Claire, Carolyn
Cleveland, Ohio 1936

in Cleveland. My uncle, Joe, had come to visit us from Detroit. My father's family was reunited. Joe's wife, Margaret, their five year old daughter Caroline and, of course, Adolph, his wife Florence, their son Eddie, his wife Dorothy, and daughter Claire, became part of my new family in America.

We children spoke no English and our adjustment in the weeks and months to follow was difficult. My father was also unable to speak English and had an extremely difficult time finding work. Although he had available funds from the sale of herring and cheese in New York, he had a strong work ethic and it was mandatory that he find a job or open his own business. He was offered a job as a janitor and felt extremely indignant at this limited opportunity after having been a successful businessman in Magdeburg and Scheveningen. He turned down the few menial job offers he received. Mark would rather not work and keep his dignity intact. He was concerned about what to do with his future.

After much thought and consternation, Mark decided that he would pursue a career in the building business, despite the fact that he knew virtually no English. His decision to build houses during the depression was considered outlandish as America was experiencing severe economic difficulties. He realized this but thought that at least someone had to have enough money to buy a home and, besides, he would be the only builder in Cleveland. There had been previous builders in the area until about 1933, but their businesses did not survive the impact of the Depression. The fact that my father would be the only builder in Cleveland was quite appealing to him and his conviction that he would be on the ground floor of a new business-venture made his decision to become Cleveland's only builder all the stronger.

Mark began constructing one home that he built on Beverly Street. Several weeks after its completion, he sold the house for $8,000. This house was probably the only home built in Cleveland for some time, and my father felt a twinge of success in his new venture. He was becoming more familiar with the English language, and proceded to purchase a lot in the suburb of University Heights, on Edgerton

Road. Soon he constructed a large luxury home on the lot, which was somewhat of a gamble. Surprisingly enough, the house sold for an amount in the $12,000 range - a big bundle in those days. Good fortune seemed to follow my father in his new experience as a builder in Cleveland and he was quite successful. He began a series of successful construction jobs, continuing to build in the University Heights suburb, and had numerous houses under construction at one time. He became a successful contractor and was slowly learning the language. His children were also becoming more and more Americanized. Mark had established himself in America.

Among the many new things experienced on an every day basis after we arrived in the United States was the daily newscasts which were broadcast beginning early in the morning and until late at night. Although these were experiences never before endured or enjoyed, the newscasts stand out in my mind as an important daily event. When mother and dad woke up in the morning, the first thing they did was to turn on the news on the radio and the same was the situation at night when they went to bed at 11:15 p.m. (the news began at 11:00 p.m. and it was over at 11:15 p.m.)

During the day mother listened to the radio intently to see if there were any newscasts and when she found them she nary missed a word. From 1936 on through the latter 30's many things occurred that made good listening. And, as they listened it helped them learn English. Through these newscasts, I believe as I look back, they received much of their Americanization and mastery of the English language.

I still recall that late in December 1936, when sit down strikers closed seven General Motors automobile assembly plants striking for the right to collective bargaining. Dad's great interest in this strike which plagued General Motors was something altogether new to him. Workers were demanding 25 million dollars in wage increases. This occurred only a month after we arrived in the country and Mark was unable to fully comprehend the dispute which had, at that time, badly crippled the automobile industry. Over 200,000 workers were put back to work who had previously either had part-time work or were laid off altogether when they settled the strike. It was hard for him to comprehend that the strike was costing over a million dollars a day to these workers. Since the depression was, in fact, on and work was so slack, how could these people not go to work, he reasoned. Anyway, it was a new experience and one of many learning scenarios which followed. About a month later, after the General Motors strike, 60,000 workers at the Chrysler plant agreed to go back to work as John L. Lewis, the head of the Committee for Industrial Organization negotiated a deal. So it went in an industrial nation, Mark reasoned. Surely there was much to learn.

Another report of daily interest concerned Amelia Earhardt having been lost at sea on her round trip around the world. Mother was very much interested in the news about the concentration camps being built in Germany and as these bits of news filtered through, she was most attentive and brought them up at the evening meal almost daily. Other news of the day, very shortly after our arrival in this country, was the British restriction of Jewish access to Palestine and many other daily events that caused great interest in our home.

It is not my belief that dad had ever considered taking the family to Palestine. Nevertheless, Palestine was very much on his mind and on mother's mind. When news of this nature was heard, it became an exciting event in the Wallach household. News was always sought about happenings in Germany. In late 1937 the Nazis began taking children from parents who refused to teach them Nazi ideology. The parents, who were pacifists, members of the Christian sect called the International Bible Researchers, had refused teaching Nazism and the court accused them of creating an environment where the children would grow up as enemies of the state. Thus, the children were taken and delivered into state care. This bit of news upset Mark and Lena very much as one of the judges delivered a lengthy statement which read in part, "The law as a racial and national instrument entrusts German parents with the education of their children only under certain conditions, namely, that they educate them in the fashion that the nation and state expect." Since apparently violations of this occurred, these people, lost their children to the state. It was very harsh treatment and it upset our family quite a bit.

Lowell Thomas, at the time, was America's premier newscaster and as I recall, his program was broadcast daily late in the afternoon at 5:45 p.m. We usually sat down to eat dinner at that time and hush was the word as he came on the air. In March of 1938 almost a year and half after our arrival in Cleveland, one evening Lowell Thomas' report shocked the family with the information that the Nazis had taken Austria. This was on March 14 of that year. The German leader, Adolph Hitler, was cheered by thousands as he returned to Vienna. This news was extremely upsetting to my mother because Vienna, Austria had been her home throughout her youth. After her depression of seeing Germany falling under Hitler's clutches, she was once again experiencing the same trauma as Hitler took her native Vienna and the rest of Austria under his wing.

The year of 1938 was not an easy one for the family, nor had 1937 been easy. It was around this time that mother and dad were both beginning to understand the newspaper and we read the Cleveland Press on a daily basis. "The Press" was an afternoon paper and it pretty well meshed and intermingled with the happenings of the day that were always heard on the radio. It was with these two sources of information that the family was kept abreast of world happenings. There were likely not many families in Cleveland at that time that were more up-to-date with the news and world happenings including the China-Japanese war, than were Mark and Lena Wallach.

There was no such thing as recreation, tennis, golf and similar activities which so many of us enjoy today. It appears to me in retrospect that the intensive study of current events through the radio and newspaper on a daily basis took the place of any recreational activity in which Mark and Lena may otherwise have participated. Nevertheless, the interest they had in all of the current world happenings was nourishing and totally satisfying to them and served as a distraction from the duties that Mark had taken on in building homes and making a living in his newly adopted country.

Of course there was no shortage of interesting news since these times were forerunners of the greatest debacle that had hit modern society in hundreds of years. As they sought information about Germany, their former homeland, they were never disappointed by a shortage from journalists. The pot was boiling and to one as interested, knowledgeable and up-to-date with current happenings as my father was, it was quite evident that the explosions of social order that he predicted over the past few years were coming to fruition. This was a pre-war era with rumblings so loud that the alert bystander surely was given sufficient fodder to know that it could not continue forever.

My Aunt Florence was helpful in aiding the Wallach family in their Americanization. She was a strong influence on my parents and helped guide the children toward American ways. By 1938, it was obvious that my father's dire predictions for Europe were turning into a grim reality. Lena was in constant touch with her sisters in Vienna and Mark with his brothers in Chorostkow and in Tarnopol. One day my parents received a postcard from Vienna, and my mother learned of her father's death. This began a period of grief and mourning for her which lasted several weeks.

Letters arrived from my father's brothers in Tarnopol, advising him of the oppressive conditions. He was told that the Ukrainians had become more and more Anti-Semitic and how the family and other Jewish people in the town were suffering. My father's "paranoia" and predictions concerning the Nazis were now quite prophetic, particularly as it related to his family in Galicia and he feared greatly for their safety.

In Nuremberg, Adolph Hitler unveiled new laws that stated categorically that Jews were not German citizens, and, therefore, could not vote nor participate in German politics. In addition, the law stated that violators would be sentenced to prison terms. The Reich had placed the swastika on its new official flag and anti-Semitism there was now part of everyday life. The Civil War in Spain was the harbinger of events in Europe. Thousands of civilians were killed in Spain by

Mark's brother Isaac (Ichtoe), his son and daughter in
Tarnopol a few months before being killed by the Nazis 1941

German war planes that swept out of the skies, strafing marketplaces and farmhouses. Small towns burned. Junkers and Heinkel bombers were practicing for what was to become World War II.

Noble Peace Prize Winner, Thomas Mann, addressed the American Guild for German Cultural Freedom in New York, calling for an end to Nazi oppression of artistic freedom. Mann had been living in Switzerland, in exile, since the authorities objected to his criticism of Nazism. He charged the German government with erasing previous culture and suppressing new forms of expression. Mann found one redeeming characteristic of the Nazi oppression - it reawakened many to the fundamental truth that the spirit must be free to be interesting. Much publicity surrounded Mann's statement.

In America, things were not much better as Father Coughlin, the radio priest of the radical right and self-proclaimed apostle of the poor, defended a broadcast he delivered in Newark, New Jersey, claiming that the Russian Revolution in 1917 was financed by the Jews.

Such allegations were seen to be common fodder among far right-wing politicians and bigoted thinkers who equated both Communism and Jews with the Devil. Coughlin, who had both rabid supporters and vehement opponents, had also attacked President Roosevelt, claiming that the President had done too little to help America's poor. The anti-Semitism he spewed was distressful and frightened my mother, Lena, severely. The rest of the family was also aroused, as it all sounded so much like Nazi Germany rhetoric.

CHAPTER 14

A NEW ERA

In March 1938, Kurt von Schuschnigg, the Premier of Austria, was invited to Berchtesgaden, Hitler's mountaintop retreat overlooking Salzburg, Austria. Berchtesgaden was also known as "Ober Salzburg" (above Salzburg). This was the beautiful retreat to which Kurt von Schuschnigg was invited to meet with Hitler regarding the Anschluss (annexation in German). What Hitler always wanted to do was to annex Austria, his birthplace, to Germany as Austria was also a German-speaking country. Von Schuschnigg decried Hitler's idea, and returned to Austria. He resigned his position to avoid the fate that met his predecessor Dolphuss. Most likely if Schuschnigg remained in office, he would have been murdered by Hitler as Dolphuss was. He was obviously aware of this and stepped out graciously avoiding a calamity that would have followed. This opened the door to the Austrian takeover.

Hitler, having left Austria in his youth as a penniless artist, was cheered by thousands as he returned to Vienna to announce the "Anschluss" or union of the country with Germany. Hitler was driven to the Austrian capital from Linz where he had set up his temporary headquarters. Forty tanks led the way and police cars filled with officers brought up the rear. Along the route, Nazis from all over Austria cheered the man who once pledged Austrian borders were inviable. Hitler stood in the open car for most of the drive, wearing his brown storm trooper uniform and returning the nearly hysterical salutes of his ardent supporters. Many of them waved banners emblazoned with swastikas. Some of the Nazis had stitched the symbol into the middle of the Austrian flag. Hitler had already signed a decree not only making himself commander-in-chief of the armed forces of Germany but also Austria. All soldiers in Austria were mandated to swear allegiance to the Nazi leader who was now the Fuhrer of 70 million people. Hitler's victory was Chancellor Kurt von Schuschnigg's defeat.

Since 1934 the Austrian chancellor had tried to prevent the national socialists from coming to power but the ground was cut out from under him when his benefactors allied himself with Hitler a couple of years earlier. Schuschnigg tried to save his government by calling for a referendum so that the Austrians could choose between the Nazis and him. The roll was never held. Hitler had contacted Austria's Nazi minister Arthur Seyss-Inquart and ordered him to have the referendum canceled. Schuschnigg had tried to resist but capitulated when he heard that German troops were massing on his border.

The Gestapo, under the command of Heinrich Himmler, said they tried to arrest Chancellor Kurt Von Schuschnigg at his house near Potsdam. Police stated he and his wife were both killed when they tried to resist. This was untrue. Other officials and storm trooper leaders were executed and some committed suicide.

Adolph Hitler destroyed all resistance after crushing efforts to hold the referendum calling for a choice for or against the Nazis.

He then held his own referendum on the union of Germany and Austria and won handily. More than 99 percent of the voters in the two countries reportedly approved the Anschluss. One prominent Austrian campaigned against Hitler. Otto de Hapsburg, a descendant of the Austrian rulers, called on the rest of the world to react against what he called German aggression in his country. Hapsburg did his campaigning outside Germany in French newspapers. A warrant had been issued for his arrest in his native Austria but he was not to be found.

In Czechoslovakia Adolph Hitler's troops fanned out throughout the Sudetenland on October 5, 1938 occupying the hotly disputed border area of that country. Hitler himself was treated as a national hero as he arrived in Eger. It looked just like Austria all over again as large crowds waved Nazi banners and threw flowers as they greeted the Fuhrer. Konrad Heinlein, the local Nazi official who helped Hitler destabilize the government of Eduard Benes welcomed the German leader. "We are happy because no longer do we have to accept a regime strange and hostile to us but one that is a part of ourselves." He stated further, "It is now a section of your homeland that greets you." The road to Eger was paved when British and French resistance to Hitler's designs on Czechoslovakia collapsed in Munich. President Roosevelt and Benito Mussolini had both urged Neville Chamberlain and Edouard Daladier to do whatever they could to avoid a new war. Czech officials had not even been invited to Munich. France decided to overlook its treaty with Prague and thus Hitler received all he wanted. He agreed to a plebiscite after his troops occupied the Sudetenland, apparently however, it was never held. Poland and Hungary stated that they would reclaim parts of Czechoslovakia that they insisted belonged to them and they, too, took their pound of flesh.

Big news in late 1938 was the "Krystalnacht." Throughout Berlin and the rest of Germany, anti-Semitism exploded as young Nazis went on rampages killing Jews at random, destroying their stores and setting fire to all the Synagogues. In Berlin itself 90 people were killed, mostly Jewish merchants.

Thousands of store windows throughout the country were smashed. Hundreds of homes and Jewish places of worship were set on fire throughout the country. The violence was unleashed after the assassination of Ernst Von Rath, third secretary of the German Embassy in Paris. The killer was a teenage Polish Jew Herschel Grynspan. He said he was avenging the treatment of his parents in Germany. "Being a Jew is not a crime" he said, "I am not a dog - I have a right to live and the Jewish people have a right to exist on this earth. Wherever I have been, I have been chased like an animal." The men who looted and killed in Berlin were all dressed in civilian clothes but many of them wore boots normally worn with Nazi uniforms and they drove party cars. Before the night of horror Jewish leaders in Berlin tried in vain to publicize the opposition to the assassination in Paris. They were stymied. The propaganda minister had already issued a decree banning all Jewish publications.

Late that year, Adolph Hitler promoted himself to be the military chief. He resolved the escalating tensions between his cabinet and the army by giving himself unprecedented power. The Fuhrer named himself supreme commander of the German Armed Forces and seized direct control of all foreign policy. Hitler had forced two generals to take early retirement. The scandal surrounding one of them, Field Marshal and War Minister Werner Von Blomberg helped to hasten the crisis. Von Blomberg was married just the previous month and Hitler himself was a witness. Since the wedding, charges had been flying that his wife was a former prostitute. General Werner Von Fritsch, Commander in Chief of the Army, was also forced to retire. He had been accused of being a homosexual. Two generals, Wilhelm Keitel and Walther Brauchitsch, had been promoted to replace them. Hitler established a secret cabinet council to advise him of foreign policies and had named several old cronies to the group including Rudolph Heshermanghering and Joachim von Ribbentrop.

Simultaneously, dispatches from Berlin said that the Nazis, who were in total control of Germany, would abate their campaign against Jews, Catholics, and Reactionaries.

This proved to be untrue, and it became evident that problems of a major nature were brewing in Germany. Terror had gripped Berlin's fashionable Kurfurstendanm District, as Jews, with blood pouring down their faces, fled from gangs of Nazi bullies who chased them shouting, "Destruction To Jews." Any cooperation of Germans with Jews would bring punishment from the government. Towns in the Cologne District forbid Jews to settle there, and one town had declared that purchases made from Jews would be considered treason to the people. Jewish mail-order houses went out of business as patrons feared to receive their parcels. Under Alfred Rosenberg's orders, boycotts reached minor services such as those provided by barbers, and the arrest of "race defilers" was not uncommon. In Breslau, charges were brought against 24 Jews and Aryan girls. They were taken away to concentration camps, the males to Lichtenberg and the females to Maurian. This was due to apparent fraternization. Mark's views were no longer that far-fetched, paranoid or crazy. My mother now realized that life in Europe was not going to go smoothly, as she had hoped it would.

In looking back, it almost appears that my father's prophesies were like an outline and were on schedule. It was the prediction of the terror and his insight into the Nazi mind, now an almost realistic and eerie phenomenon of seeing into the future. What Mark had said would take place, in fact, did take place, almost as he had predicted. It is almost that he was a psychic with superhuman powers. Surely this is not what he wanted to see, but it was almost totally accurate to what he said was going to be. The tragedy of "Krystalnacht" was not to be forgotten for years to come and may not be forgotten for hundreds of years yet to be. Hitler and his Nazi Germany had shown their true colors for all to see. No time in the near or far off future could any doubts or illusions exist of ideology or intent.

CHAPTER 15

PRE-WAR

On March 15, 1939, with startling efficiency, Adolph Hitler arrived triumphantly in Prague, just eight hours after the first German troops entered what used to be the capital of the Czechoslovakian Republic. The country was now divided into several regions, all of them obedient to Adolph Hitler. The swastika was flown above the castles of the Bohemian kings, and the Germans cheered the Fuhrer's arrival. Hitler's arrival in Czechoslovakia was not so majestic as his previous conquests of Austria and the Sudetenland. Many Czechs who did not claim a German heritage jeered as the soldiers of the Reich took over. Others hid down side streets and wept openly. East Slovkia was now also being dominated by the Germans. The Prime Minister of the area, Monsignor Joseph Tiso, struck a deal with Hitler two days after Czech

President Emile Hacha tried to arrest him. Hacha tried earlier that month to dissolve the autonomous government of Carpathos Ukraine. This area was invaded by Hungarian troops reportedly with the blessing and full backing of Hitler. Throughout Prague, a curfew went into effect and public buildings and banks were taken over by Germans. The Gestapo was fanning out throughout the city carrying "lists," as Jews became the hunted prey, with many Czechs aiding Hitler's S.S. in seeking them out.

In May, Germany signed the "Pact of Steel" as it was called. One of the most grandiose alliances in modern history was consummated when Italy and Germany created the invincible block which was to become known as the Axis. The axis powers signed this "Pact of Steel" that bound them economically, politically and militarily with a declared objective of organizing Europe, promoting the two powerful nations and creating a "just peace" in the world. At the signing ceremony, present were top German officials, including Chancellor Hitler who agreed that Germany would rule on land and Italy on sea in times of war which Europeans saw lurking on the horizon. Britain was alarmed by the event and called an extra session of Parliament to discuss the pact's ramifications. Although war did not break out until September 1, 1939, raw nerves and fiery rhetoric ruled the presses and airwaves. On July 30, the latest flash point of tension in Europe was the hotly disputed strategic city of Danzig. Adolph Hitler was making it quite clear he wanted to absorb Danzig into the Reich. France and Britain had both warned him the action could hasten another war. The warnings were contained in separate statements by the French Foreign Minister and the British Prime Minister. Both men told Hitler that they expect him to respect the status of Danzig as mandated by the Versailles Treaty. The warnings were the strongest yet to the Fuhrer but he showed no signs of heeding them. His military commanders had already assembled a strike force of tanks and cavalry that could easily be used in an invasion of Danzig and the arm of Poland known as the "Corridor" which stretches into the Baltic.

Further south, Italian forces invaded the tiny Balkan kingdom of Albania. There was little resistance and King Zog was chased from the throne. He took asylum in Greece, which was only one of many countries nervous about the intentions of Benito Mussolini. The invasion was carried out swiftly and without any warning from Rome. A spokesman for Mussolini said he ordered the troop movement to protect Italian residents in Albania who have been threatened by roving armed bands. Italy and Albania had been conducting peace negotiations but King Zog was resisting Mussolini's military demands. Il Duce insisted that his navy be given permanent access to Albanian harbors and that army garrisons be established along Albania's border with Greece and Yugoslavia.

Count Galeazzo Ciano, Benito Mussolini's son-in-law, and Italy's foreign minister, met with Yugoslav ambassador Bosko Hristic and assured him that Mussolini had no designs on his country. Yugoslavian diplomats said privately they were satisfied with these assurances.

While this was happening in the Balkan arena, Prime Minister Neville Chamberlain had pledged to support Poland militarily against threats to her sovereignty. The official statement issued from London declared, "Should the Polish Government feel that its independence would be threatened to such an extent that it had to resist by force, Poland would find Britain and France at her side."

Realizing the British statement referred to German aggression, Chancellor Adolph Hitler accosted England, challenging her to pick a fight or stop interfering with the Reich's political aspirations. In a ceremony launching the 35,000 ton battleship, Admiral Von Tirpitz, Hitler spoke with fervent anger to 100,000 at Wilhelmshaven. He warned that Germany would not allow Britain to initiate a "devilish plan" of encirclement used prior to the war. He proclaimed to the crowd, "Whoever declares himself ready to pull the chestnuts out of the fire of the big powers must expect to burn his fingers in the attempt." Observers called the speech, "uncharacteristically confused."

The Nazis and the Communists made friends and shook hands in Moscow on August 23, 1939 as they shocked the leaders of the western world. Germany and the Soviet Union had signed a non aggression treaty that stymied efforts in Paris and London to restrain Hitler. The pact was signed by German Foreign Minister Joachim von Ribbentrop, Soviet Leader Joseph Stalin and his Commissioner of Foreign Affairs, Vyacheslav Molotov. The treaty was approved less than a week after the country signed a trade agreement in Berlin. The non aggression treaty was being praised in Berlin as an enormous victory over British efforts to form a circle around Germany with the help of friends in Russia. Stalin was never very comfortable with the British and they were never very comfortable with him said Hitler. This treaty of course isolated Poland and eastern Europe and a diplomatic maneuvering indicated Hitler was as determined as ever to annex Danzig and extract corridor concessions from Warsaw. German commanders were to prepare for immediate military actions and the new military treaty gave Hitler more freedom to march as Germany mobilized all its forces.

While Europe teetered precariously, the world of tomorrow was unveiled at the New

York World's Fair. President Franklin Roosevelt formally dedicated the exposition at a speech delivered to 600,000 listeners huddled in a chilly breeze. The President's speech was climaxed by a parade through the 1,216 acre grounds. Nearly 20,000 armed servicemen marched, joined by people from Europe, Asia, and the Americas clad in native costumes. Those who truly made the fair possible were the workmen and they also marched past the steel ball that was the center of the attractions. A statue of George Washington stood in the stands on Constitution Mall. The Hall of Nations featured the Soviet Pavilion.

A happening on the west coast made the country agog as Barbara Stanwick, 31, a popular American screen heroine, married Robert Taylor, four years her junior, at the home of friends in San Diego. They obtained the marriage license by using their true names of Ruby Stevens and Faye Arlington Spangler Brugh. They kept their plan a secret and postponed the wedding trip until they finished making a movie with Heddy Lamarr.

Back in Europe, the Jews were fearful

for their lives and with good reason. Persecution in Germany was rampant. The ship, the St. Louis, left Germany and traveled from port-to-port with its many Jewish passengers seeking refuge from anti-Semitism. The 979 Jewish refugees from Germany with 400 women and children aboard this Hamburg-American line were denied admission to Cuba. The Cuban government declared that 9,300 refugees were already on the island, and the economic conditions allowed no more. Appeals were made to the President and Congress of the U.S. to provide asylum. The appeals were refused. There were attempted suicides by those aboard the St. Louis as other refugee ships sought haven unsuccessfully. The plight of the Jews in Germany became a major problem. A plan to settle 30,000 refugees in the Philippines was being discussed. Nothing ever came of this plan. Mark Wallach's predictions of hell on earth were being realized, and others with whom he had shared his predictions marveled at his foresight. I marveled at his foresight, as well, but at age 13 did not grasp the full meaning of his genius, his foresight and his intestinal fortitude to act when action was needed, yet so difficult. At this writing it is so much more appreciated.

During this bleak period, Mark continued to urge his brothers still living in the Ukraine to come to the United States. He was unable to get them to leave their homes, however. Apparently in this country, Mark got more accurate news of what was happening in the world than what his brothers heard in the Ukraine. The S.S. now had mobile killing squads, manned by Germans, Ukrainians, and Poles in the region where members of the Wallach family still lived. As time went on, news finally spread throughout the Ukraine of what was really happening as these killing squads murdered hundreds and thousands of Jews. One day, a postcard arrived from my Uncle Moses from Chorostkow, saying that this would be "our last communique" from him because he was expecting the worst. Sadly to say, his assessment was accurate of the conditions there. Within several months, every member of Mark's family was killed in both Tarnopol and Chorostkow. All were murdered by killing squads except two sisters from the "Winter" part of our family. These two teenaged girls were sent to the concentration camp, Auschwitz, at Oswiecim, Poland. As inmates there, they were recruited by Dr. Joseph Mengele who conducted medical experiments on them testing pain tolerance. Both girls survived the war and were freed by the Russian Army. Their physical and mental conditions were such that they would be classified as "vegetables," or living, mindless corpses. Both were eventually sent to Israel where they were institutionalized, never to recover. Both died during the 1980's, never having really lived at all, their lives having been snuffed out by the "Angel of Death," Joseph Mengele.

Lena's family in Vienna fared much better. Osias Lopater, Lena's father, had died on April 20, 1937 and Mark persuaded Elsie, Lena's youngest sister who had lived with Osias, to come to the United States. Mark worked diligently in trying to persuade his brother-in-law, Max, married to Lena's oldest sister, Jetty, to emigrate to the United States. Max and Jetty's two sons were already in America, having been brought here from Vienna by a family in Boston. Still, Max and

Jetty couldn't be convinced to come to America. Regie, Lena's younger sister, and her physician-husband, Willie, were also being persuaded by Mark to come to America. Mark met with resistance from Max, Jetty, Regie and Willie. They did not want to leave Vienna. Unfortunately, Mark soon learned that the Nazis had arrested Willie and thrown him in jail. He was likely headed for the concentration camp at Mathausen, not far from Vienna. Through some miracle, Mark obtained Willie's release from jail. Even at this point, Willie refused to come to America and made demands of Mark that he and Regie would come only if accompanied by a Dr. Deutsch and his wife, their close friends. Mark managed to bring them all to the United States - Willie, Regie, and their son, Heinz, together with Dr. Deutsch and his wife. At the same time, Mark convinced Max and Jetty to come to this country and join their sons, Robert and Fred, who were now in Boston. It was felt that if they remained even for a few days longer in Vienna, they would surely have been taken away to concentration camps and certain death. Mark knew better than the Viennese family, who refused to believe even until the last moment.

At this point, Elsie had come to live with our family. She had obtained a job in a bakery practicing her art of making fine strudel. The bakery came to appreciate Elsie's talents, and she began to make a living for herself in her new country. Elsie was blond and beautiful. Willie, Regie's physician-husband, had a difficult time here. He was an aristocrat, a proud and stiff Austrian who looked down upon the American heathens who were asking him to pass exams before allowing him to practice medicine. Willie finally did take and pass his medical exams and became an "in house" doctor for a railroad company. He soon opened a small practice of his own as well.

Tremendous rivalries grew between my mother and her sisters who were always fighting and would not talk to each other for years on end. Max opened a costume jewelry business, eking out a living.

Mark saw the United States getting into war production and the "lend-lease programs."

The steel mills in Elyria and Lorain, Ohio were booming, and he felt that housing for the factory workers would be in great demand. He was able to secure a government contract to build houses on land surrounding the factories. The houses cost approximately $6,000-$7,000 each, and his construction business continued to thrive with the addition of these new projects. Mark was dedicated to building quality homes. He felt that if his name was going to be on a house, his reputation would suffer if the work was shoddy. He was good to people and his workers. Even years later, if there was some question concerning the workmanship on one of his homes, he would make every effort to make it good. He was a businessman from the old school - a handshake to him was as good as the tightest contract. His reputation was impeccable and he was proud of it.

As a quality builder who took so much pride in his work, Mark found it a little bit difficult building the "hurry up and get finished" defense houses, as they were called, around the Elyria and Lorain factories. The quality of work that was required here was not what he had been used to in University Heights and, at times, he found it difficult staying within the price range that was demanded and yet, at the same time, maintaining the type of quality to which he had been accustomed in the past couple of years. Compromise was ever present and he did his best.

In addition to the "quality - price" problem that Mark faced, there was also the gasoline rationing problem which beset the country. Gasoline rationing had gone into effect on a nationwide basis in the United States, a move which affected 27 million passenger cars and 5 million buses and trucks in an effort to conserve both gas and rubber tires. Some 7 million auto owners in 13 eastern states had already had a taste of such restrictions, having been limited to 3 gallons of gas per week. Under a new plan embracing the entire nation, car owners would only get 4 gallons of gas per week. President Roosevelt had ordered this measure and the rationing of coffee as well and both took effect. The country established a war petroleum administration which was to govern the gasoline shortage dilemma.

Somehow Mark always found it possible to do the impossible and though Elyria and Lorain were 40 and 50 miles, respectively, west of our home in University Heights, he managed with a little pull here and little pull there to get the extra gasoline needed so that he could be on the job on a daily basis and see to it that the homes, which were so badly needed for the defense workers, were made ready for them.

The depression had now come to a slow halt as the country counted 131 million people in its 1940 census. While the stork flew in through 6,000 windows and 4,000 souls departed monthly, 120,000 enumerators asked questions in order to clarify the needs in housing and schools and to give legislators facts for laws dealing with unemployment and relief. The average household was 3.8 persons and the median age was 28.9 years. The decade gain was the smallest in the country's history due to the low birth rate.

As the year progressed, Winston Churchill, a constant critic of Britain's policy of appeasement of Adolph Hitler, walked proudly into the House of Commons to give his first speech to the nation as the new Prime Minister. "I have nothing to offer," Churchill said, "but blood, toil, tears and sweat." Churchill was asked by King George VI, three days prior, to form a new government after Neville Chamberlain had resigned. Chamberlain was forced out under mounting pressure from labor and his own conservative party. It was believed, at first, that the crisis generated by Hitler's invasion of Belgium would create new support for Chamberlain. The invasion actually served to fuel criticism of him. Chamberlain will always be remembered as the architect of appeasement at Munich. Churchill had become the symbol of British resistance to Hitler. He had served as the First Lord of the Admiralty under Chamberlain. Despite the ill feelings toward Chamberlain, he was expected to serve in the new government of Winston Churchill.

During this ominous period, with the United States fearing consequences of events in Europe, President Roosevelt, in an effort to prepare for the very worst, direct involvement of America in the European conflict, announced plans to train 50,000 volunteer airplane pilots. The extensive training program would draw men from colleges, where the Civil Aeronautics Authority provided courses, from citizens who already had private airplane licenses and from those who simply wanted to join up.

Congress passed a defense bill that expanded the Army Air Corps. in support of Franklin Roosevelt's proposal.

There was much strife in the country as the public appeared to be choosing sides with a strong pro-Nazi movement being countered by a much stronger and forceful population supporting the British and the French. Also very much in the forefront were thousands, and possibly several million isolationists who did not want this country to get involved at all, either by shipping war goods to the allies or, least of all, getting involved militarily.

CHAPTER 16

THE WAR YEARS

On September 1, 1939, after 20 years of tenuous peace, Europe was again at war. A mighty German force of 1.25 million men swept across the Polish border. On September 17, Russian troops pushed in from the east. Poland recoiled in the clutches of defeat. The German invasion came without the declaration of war and was executed by General Walter von Brauchitsch, who easily led his troops and tank brigades over the dry, warm Polish terrain. As the assault stormed on, Nazi Chief of State, Albert Forster, proclaimed the annexation of the free city of Danzig to the Third Reich. Forster told the people of Danzig, "Our Fuhrer, Adolph Hitler, has freed us." Now the German flag flew over the city, capping months of Nazi planning. After Hitler's government ignored an ultimatum from Great Britain and France to withdraw its troops or face Anglo-French involvement of the conflict, the two Western nations declared war against Germany, fulfilling the defense obligations with Poland. Russian troops met advancing German forces on September 18 after they easily trounced Polish defenders. Plans were made for the partition of Poland. Ten days later, Soviet Leader, Joseph Stalin, met with Foreign Minister Vyacheslav Molotov and German Foreign Minister Joachim von Ribbentrop in Moscow for the German-Soviet Agreement to divide the beleaguered nation. According to a communique released by the two aggressors, troops will occupy Poland to "bring order to Poland and help the Polish people confronted with the collapse of their state."

The territorial division granted the Soviets some 76,500 square miles of Poland's eastern region, with an approximate population of 12.8 million people. Germany received a sphere of influence encompassing Lublin in the east, and most of the western portion of the country, including the capital of Warsaw, a city devastated by three weeks of nightmarish bombing.

The German campaign had exhibited the power, speed, and determination of a well trained and innovative military. Its blitzkrieg or lightening war, impressed international observers who remembered the failed trench warfare of German forces during World War I. The invasion elicited condemnation by almost every sovereign state. Finland appealed to the League of Nations to expel Russia from membership, which it did. In the United States, President Roosevelt pledged to keep America out of a European war that could be long and deadly. His answer to reporters' inquiries, asking if the U.S. could keep out of the war, was "I not only sincerely hope so, but I believe we can and every effort will be made to do so."

Meanwhile, confronted with the destruction of their nation, the Poles continued to bleed mercilessly. An estimated 60,000 Poles had been killed within two weeks after the Nazi invasion began, approximately 200,000 had been wounded, and 700,000 soldiers were being held in captivity. In some circles, Polish ineptitude was blamed for the tragic and great loss of life, yet credit must be given to the fierce and impassioned German forces held spellbound by dictator Adolph Hitler. The high degree of German discipline made the Polish military appear to be at least a war behind.

Questions remained as to how long the German-Russian alliance was to last. Close Nazi-Soviet relations had persisted since May of 1939, but the two powers were now neighbors since Poland no longer served as a buffer zone. The two nations now had other problems to work out which arose from the partitioning of Poland.

1939 was the harbinger of things to come. The Wallach family, now safely ensconced in Cleveland, Ohio, was shocked at the happenings in Europe. Mark, without ever mentioning "I told you so" was grief-stricken by what was happening to his homeland. The Wallach family lived comfortably in University Heights, an upscale suburb of Cleveland, Ohio. Mark had built a beautiful family home on Edgerton Road, the same street where he began his construction business two years earlier. The three children continued to adjust to life in America. I was athletically inclined and active in football, basketball, tennis and baseball during my school years until inducted into the Navy. My mother was quite devoted to our family, but unfortunately, she and her sisters remained estranged from each other. They rarely saw each other and there was a constant state of siege among them.

Blood indelibly stained European soil after Great Britain and France declared war on Germany following the Nazi's lightening invasion of Poland. Immediately after German troops blistered across the Polish border, the French and British governments issued an ultimatum to the Third Reich. "Suspend all aggressive action against Poland and withdraw from Polish territory or the United Kingdom and France, in fulfillment of our obligation, will come to Poland's assistance." After two days of Germany's penetration toward Warsaw, on September 3, 1939, British Prime Minister Neville Chamberlain made his fateful and, to many, inevitable, declaration that the two western powers would fight Adolph Hitler's troops. "We shall be fighting against brute force," the British leader added. The obligations Chamberlain referred to were mutual defense treaties that Poland, France and England had signed previously.

Great Britain quickly announced a blockade of Germany upon entering the war. Germany retaliated when one of its submarines attacked and sank a British passenger liner, The Athenia, on its route from Liverpool to Montreal as 112 people perished in the assault. The first British attack occurred on September 4, when the English Air Force bombed the German fleet at the North Sea entrance to the Kiel Canal. Many of the Reich's ships were destroyed or seriously damaged. The Germans accurately set their anti-aircraft guns and downed five English planes.

Heavy artillery fire was not the only thing unleashed from British aircraft, as Chamberlain ordered pilots to unload six million leaflets on German terrain. The leaflets were entitled, "Warning from Great Britain to the German People." They appealed to the German citizenry by explaining Britain's position in the war and forecasting a potentially long war. The leaflets described the Nazi leaders as liars, condemning the German people as mass murderers. The propaganda pamphlets implored the Germans to insist upon peace and cautioned that British strength would annihilate Germany in a protracted war.

While France and Britain declared war, scores of other nations expressed their adamant wishes to stay out of the fighting. The United States denounced the German aggression but stated it would not become engaged. President Roosevelt again said that the U.S. would remain neutral, but added, "I cannot ask that every American remain neutral in thought as well." Latin American countries as well as the Balkan states proclaimed their intentions to remain aloof from the war. In Italy, the course had been set for non-involvement so decidedly that Italian trade ships resumed their normal sea commerce despite the presence of German submarines.

German U-Boat warfare had been very effective that first month of the war. On September 7, Nazi submarines sank or fired upon seven French and British vessels, including the British vessels, The Manaar and The Corinthic, and the French vessel, The Tammare. There were at least two people dead and forty reported missing from the assault on The Manaar. According to eye witnesses, four torpedoes struck the British freighter - the fourth broke her in half. By mid-month, 19 Allied ships had been blasted to the bottom of the sea by Nazi submarines. The French had mobilized eight million soldiers, many sent to fortify the West Wall. Earlier that month, the French made contact with their German opponents, but most Nazi troops were located in the East, expanding their conquest of Poland. Some military observers believed a French offensive into Germany might deflate the Reich's strategic momentum, but no moves were made other than the policies of blockading Germany and defensive preparations. Meanwhile, all the world worried as to when the temporary calm on the Western Front would erupt.

President Roosevelt continued to proclaim United States neutrality concerning the war in Europe and moved toward holding a Pan American parley to cushion the Western hemisphere against the ravages of war. In one proclamation, he denied access to the United States' territorial waters to belligerents engaged in the European war. In another proclamation, the President clamped an embargo on shipments of arms, munitions, airplanes, and plane parts to all those countries in which a state of war unhappily existed. These countries were France, Germany, the United Kingdom, Poland, India, Austria, and New Zealand. Canada and South Africa were not named, since the Parliaments of those British dominions had not declared war against Germany at that time. Roosevelt's proclamation of neutrality was similar to that issued by then-President Wilson at the outbreak of war in Europe in 1914, long before the U.S. entered World War I.

Adolph Hitler, bristling at the rejection of his peace offer to London and Paris, vowed that Germany would fight the war to its bitter end in Western Europe. "England and France rejected the Fuhrer's hand of peace," the German government said. "They threw down the gauntlet; Germany has taken it up." The

German government denied reports that Hitler would make another peace offer to the French. Hitler made his offer to the Reichstag earlier that month after his military victory in Poland. French Premier Daladier was the first to reject Hitler's overtures. Daladier said, "No real justice and lasting peace" would be possible until Hitler is defeated. President Roosevelt also turned down an indirect appeal from Hitler to mediate an end to the war.

Hitler was furious at the new treaty among Britain, France, and Turkey. He warned Turkey that it was playing with fire and he held urgent meetings concerning this latest development.

With the war in Poland over quickly, attention focused on the front between Germany and France which was unexpectedly quiet until the spring of 1940. The Maginot Line extending from the northern border of Spain to Belgium had been reinforced and was laden with troops underground ready to annihilate any frontal attack from the Germans who were equally hidden in the Ziegfried Line not too far to the east. Pillbox after pillbox of the Maginot Line faced pillbox after pillbox on the Ziegfried Line. The German government had built the Ziegfried Line after World War I very similar to the Maginot Line, a defensive line with underground passages. These lines facing each other were supposedly impenetrable. There was as much as a half mile of depth in some of the areas and supposedly each side would be unable to cross the other's line. In the spring of 1940 Germany sent its army through Belgium and Holland to avoid the Maginot Line. The German army came into France through the Ardennes Forest to the north of the French border. The mutual fighting of a war had now begun as the Dutch, Belgian, French and German armies and air forces for the first time in eight months began to battle with a fury unleashed that had not been seen since the declaration of war eight months earlier.

While this was happening, more than 800 soldiers aboard the British battleship, The Royal Oak, were believed dead after a German submarine's torpedo struck and sank the Admiralty's ship. It was a particularly surprising event since most of Great Britain's

Admiralty thought that the ship's bulging armor would repel a torpedo. It did not and only 396 members of the crew survived the tragedy.

During the following months, reports of torture and other atrocities inflicted upon the Jews by the Nazis filtered out of Germany. There were reports detailing the destruction and looting of Jewish businesses and homes by orders of the Nazis. Other reports cited the burning of synagogues, the flogging of Jews with barbed-wire birches, and brutal killings during 1938, 1939 and 1940. In the Buchenwald camp, physical labor far beyond human capacity was the order of the day. Many were forced to do knee bends while holding huge stone blocks. There was the discovery of "tree binding" and "merry-go-rounding." A victim's arms would be bound around a tree with his feet barely touching the ground. Kicks and blows reigned upon the victim generating a macabre dance. The sweatbox guaranteed a slow, agonizing death. A document called "The White Paper" provided insight into these dark days of horrible torture during what was perhaps one of the dimmest period recorded in the annals of history.

Meanwhile, in the United States, "Mr. Smith Goes To Washington," the latest Frank Capra romp opened at New York City's Radio Music Hall. The film was a humorous swipe at the U.S. Senate with an underlying "get you in the gut" patriotism. It was similar to Capra's "Mr. Deeds Goes To Town," which focused on a naive fellow who aimed to make everyone as happy as possible. Jimmy Stewart's Mr. Smith, like Gary Cooper's Mr. Deeds, was drawling and earnest. He reacted to a filibuster's hidden clauses and political intrigue with stuttering horror. Claude Raines portrayed a senior Senator who showed Smith the ropes.

Also here at home, rebel yells greeted the premiere of "Gone With the Wind" in Atlanta. The film, based on Margaret Mitchell's sweeping novel of the Civil War South had passed its most difficult test. Would Atlanta view the Technicolor torching of its own city as a smear on Southern honor? Judging by the whoops and hollers of the

231

crowd, the reply was a resounding "Hell No!" The Atlanta Grand Theater was redesigned that evening to resemble Twelve Oaks, the Hamilton plantation where Scarlett O'Hara and her many beaus dallied. At 6 p.m., the theater was roped off to keep happy fans from crushing the stars of the film as they arrived in their limousines. Clark Gable put in an appearance at 8:40 p.m. A few women fainted at the sight of him. Miss Mitchell gave a speech when the 3-hour, 45-minute film epic ended. In a quivering tone, she said it was a great thing for Georgia and the South to see the Confederates come home. Mrs. Dorothy Lamour, the great actress and President of the United Daughters of the Confederacy, praised the casting of Vivien Leigh as Scarlett. No one could equal her. Vivien Leigh was Margaret Mitchell's Scarlett come to life.

In South America, the commander of the German battleship Graf Spee, Captain Langsdorff, scuttled his craft off Montevideo and placed a revolver to his head and fired. A deadly sea battle with the British cruisers, Exeter, Ajax, and Achilles, had mostly destroyed it, killing many crew members as well as destroying the morale of the survivors and its skipper. The British squadron, under the leadership of Commodore H.H. Harwood, opened fire on the German battleship after the Graf Spee had attacked the Ajax. The German ship, with its swiftness and heavy armaments, held off the three Royal Navy vessels for hours but received numerous hits. Finally, after a day's worth of battling, she limped into the Montevideo harbor, seriously damaged, with 36 crew members dead and 60 wounded. On orders from Adolph Hitler, Langsdorff blew up what had been one of the greatest ships in the German fleet.

Russia and Finland continued their war which began in November of 1939. The skies over Finland had cleared in mid-January. Russian bombers punished civilian populations in Helsinki and elsewhere as Russia and Finland battled fiercely in a war of attrition. The Russians seemed desperate. They had suffered large losses in a six week old war which began about the first week in December and were hell bent on teaching the Finns a lesson. Hundreds of Russians were killed in fierce fighting on the Karelian Isthmus. Soviet tanks were trapped in the snow and captured. Large numbers of prisoners were taken, many of them exhausted and suffering from frostbite as Swedish, Norwegian and Danish volunteers had been fighting with the Finns. Their governments said the Russians will not be allowed to attack Finland from their territory. Reports said that the Russians were so angry and frustrated that they were brawling in their camps. Russian pilots were said to be fighting each other in the air. Military commanders in Moscow denied these reports and those that scores of Red Army officers had been recalled to be punished. They did not deny that secret police had been dispatched to Finland to buttress the front lines.

The vicious war between Russia and Finland ended on March 13, 1940, three and a half months after it began. A Peace Treaty was signed in Moscow. Finland was forced to surrender large parts of its territory, including the Karelian Isthmus, the scene of the bloodiest fighting of the undeclared war between the Russians and the Finns. Thousands of Finnish and Russian soldiers were buried beneath the snow as Finland mourned. Under the terms of the Treaty, Finland agreed to remove most of its submarines and warships from the Arctic Ocean. Finland agreed to lease the area around Hangoe to the Russians so that they could build a military base. Meanwhile, informed sources stated that a major development of talks between Hitler and Mussolini would be the formation of a three-power entente among Germany, Italy, and Russia.

Germany had launched immediate talks with Moscow. The entente was aimed at new order in Europe by assuring political and economic homogeneity, dispersing the sphere of British influence and eliminating British influence as a political force in Southeastern Europe and, possibly, the Near East.

Distraught over President Roosevelt's foreign policy, a group of Isolationists formed the "America First" Committee. Its members included Charles Lindbergh, Robert McCormick (Publisher of the Chicago Tribune), and a few senators. The Isolationists opposed U.S. intervention in a European war and organized to protest, picket, and parade for their cause. They were diametrically opposed to the Internationalists, who felt that only by banding together could Western nations defeat Fascism.

Most non-right wing Americans were totally opposed to this "America First Committee" which appeared to hide under a patriotic name, yet, in fact, was considered by many as not a patriotic organization at all. The majority of Americans felt very strongly that the "America First Committee" was primarily composed of Nazi sympathizers, anti-Semites and was backed by many hooligan elements. My parents were shocked that such an organization could recruit so many members as well as so many well known Americans. There had surely been enough evidence over the past two years to prove beyond a shadow of a doubt the dastardly conduct displayed by the Nazis in Germany. The concentration camps were, by this time, known and recognized and the torture administered to all those who disagreed with Hitler was no longer a secret in this country. My father, as one of probably millions, was aghast that this organization gained such prominence. It was a Father Coughlin-like organization hidden behind the patriotic name of "American First" where in reality it was composed of thousands of bigots of the Ku Klux Klan variety. Luckily for the country, the organization became known for what it was after a short period of time and it waned in its prominence. The ugly bunch dissipated, never to be heard from again as the people of America recognized the organization and took the appropriate actions needed. And so, life went on in America, during the early 1940's.

CHAPTER 17

THE FIGHTING BEGINS

On May 10, 1940, the Germans launched a blitzkrieg in the low countries as hundreds of airplanes swooped over Belgium and Dutch cities and airfields. The blitzkrieg softened these countries' defenses for an invasion of German land troops as Nazis expanded their path of destruction.

In the Netherlands, German forces demonstrated the effectiveness of a blitzkrieg. Major airfields in and around Amsterdam received heavy shelling in the predawn, fast-paced attacks. German parachutists, some dressed in Dutch military uniforms, dropped from the sky as German ground troops bolted across the border. The swift assault did not take the Dutch completely by surprise. For a week, they had readied themselves for German aggression. In fact, anti-aircraft guns downed at least six German planes, but the powerful, well-balanced blitzkrieg had left the Dutch bleeding and scarred. Needless to say, war was immediately declared on Germany by the Dutch. Holland's Queen Wilhemina addressed the populace, saying, "After our country, with scrupulous conscientiousness, had observed strict neutrality, Germany made a sudden attack on our territory without warning." She asked her people to take up arms with the utmost vigilance and with that inner calm that comes from a clear conscience.

Other German brigades crossed the Belgium border in a similarly quick and effective manner. In the early morning hours, the Nazi Air Force unloaded heavy artillery on Antwerp, Nivelles and Brussels. Paratroopers landed on the mighty Fort Eban Emael, the northern fortress in the Belgium defense line. While defenders battled the Reich's sky-to-land units, German foot soldiers surged virtually untouched over the nearby Albert Canal. The Antwerp Airport was struck by a barrage of bombs that did not stop until daybreak. When the barrage ceased, 400 Belgians had been killed. Houses adjacent to the Airport burned out of control and inhabitants fled for their lives. According to German Foreign Minister Joachim von Ribbentrop, the joint invasions were ordered for the protection of the lowlands against Allied insurgents. He said the British and French were about to use the lowlands as stepping stones for an invasion into Germany. "The Allies were preparing an onslaught on Germany that the Reich could not tolerate," von Ribbentrop said. He issued the following statement, "In the life and death struggle, thrust upon the German people the government does not intend to await an attack by Britain and France." The Allied government responded by dismissing such preposterous allegations as Nazi propaganda.

Dark days arrived in Belgium shortly thereafter as King Leopold ordered the Belgian Army to capitulate to Germany. The surrender occurred against the wishes of French Premier Paul Reanaud who described the situation as dark and grave, adding, "France's faith in victory along with our Belgian alliance is still strong." The news of Belgium's surrender arrived two weeks after the Netherlands succumbed to the relentless barrage of Germany's blitzkrieg. On May 14, 1940, Dutch Commander-in-Chief, Henry Garrot Winkelman, asked his troops to surrender to Germany to prevent further bloodshed and annihilation.

While the leaders of France and Britain expressed their disdain for the acquiescence by the Dutch and Belgians, their harsh words masked their true emotions. Both Allied nations were frustrated and intimidated by the Reich's success in the lowlands. The Nazis now stood poised at the English Channel at the Somme-Aisne Line. The Allies realized that their lands were next on the Hitler invasion agenda.

To the North of Paris, the French were battling the Germans all along the Maginot Line as the Germans broke through the line at several points. The German front now extended over 300 miles from the Rhine all the way to Le Havre. Later, the Germans seized that port city and another 100 miles of the French coastline. The German victory would make England even more vulnerable. Cherbourgh was the next target the Germans would soon take.

Indeed, German victory was realized as the Allies were soundly defeated in the Battles of Northern France and, surprisingly so in less than two weeks of heavy fighting. France asked for an armistice when the German army prepared to march into Paris. The British Royal Navy led a successful exodus of 340,000 Allied troops from the seaport of Dunkirk on the shores of northern France who had faced imminent annihilation there. Throngs of cheering British greeted ships crossing the English Channel packed with battle-weary but rescued soldiers. The evacuation was considered one of Britain's greatest military achievements. In the meantime, the French wept under German control.

France fell to Germany in May of 1940 after the British surrendered the city of Dunkirk in northern France. The German Army had pinned the troops against the sea and could have annihilated them, but Hermann Goering, the highest ranking official in charge of the German Air Force, wanted to show the prowess of the German Air Force and suggested that Hitler let him "bomb the troops out." Fortunately, the bombing was a miserable failure. The British sent fighter planes to protect the troops and brought in thousands of small vessels that allowed the troops to evacuate Dunkirk.

On June 14, the French people's beloved City of Paris was no longer the City of Light. Darkness fell over the capital as German troops marched from Neuilly toward the center of Paris. German tanks paraded through the Place de la Concorde and German armored cars swept past the trees of the Champs Elysee. French men and women wept openly. Much of the city was deserted, however, as two million Parisians streamed out of the capital as the government packed up and headed to Tours before the Germans' arrival. The Germans removed French flags from government buildings and quickly replaced them with swastikas. New signs were plastered on the Eiffel Tower and the Chamber of Deputies, "Deutschland siegt an alle Fronten, " meaning, "Germany victorious on all fronts."

The French Military Command claimed it gave up Paris without much of a struggle to spare it from the fate of Warsaw. Germany snickered at the excuse and retorted that the French were powerless to defend their capital. The German High Command claimed it would occupy the rest of France within the next two weeks, and then turn its attention toward Great Britain and Winston Churchill. Those accusing the Germans of arrogance were reminded that they seized Paris just 10 days after the Battle of France began. The Germans claimed that the French were forced to abandon a large amount of military equipment when they retreated. Germany said the losses were devastating to France since they followed so closely to the disaster at Dunkirk. Germany claimed that the seizure of Paris also disrupted the economic structure of France and destroyed key communication linking the French Army.

In the meantime, back in the United States, President Roosevelt, in his graduation address at the University of Virginia, accused the Italian government of a stab in the back by aligning with Germany in the war being waged against Britain and France. On the tenth day of June 1940, the President said, "The hand that held the dagger has struck it into the back of its neighbor." In view of Italy's entry into the war, the President had said the United States would give its utmost aid to Great Britain, calling them opponents of evil force. The President spoke hours after Benito Mussolini of Italy announced his decision to join hands with Germany's Adolph Hitler, despite America's efforts to persuade Italy to stay out of the war. Roosevelt reiterated his hopes that the U.S. would soon begin compulsory military training sufficient for any defensive emergency.

A tragedy occurred in the Mediterranean that was bound to exacerbate relations between Britain and France and hurt their efforts to stop Hitler. On July 3, the British Navy opened fire and sank a large number of French ships anchored at Mers-el-kebir in Algeria. Some 1,000 French soldiers perished. Winston Churchill was concerned that French ships that had not joined General DeGaulle would be commandeered by Germany. He was not aware of an edict that the French were under orders to scuttle vessels they could not defend against the German might. The British opened fire when the French rejected an ultimatum to sail for Britain or the United States.

The Vichy government in France acted quickly to arrest and jail four prominent government officials who were charged with the defeat of France in the war. There was apparently more to this case than met the eye, for Germany was demanding that the Petain Government punish the defendants properly. Those arrested included former Premiers Leon Bloom and Edouard Daladier, Foreign Minister of War, George Mandel, who served as Minister of the Interior, and General Maurice Gamalyn, who served as Commander-in-Chief of all French forces. Defendants were tried by the new Supreme Court Justice set up by Vichy government and were condemned to death along with Charles DeGaulle, in absentia. DeGaulle, who was leading the French Resistance from London, was accused of treason, plotting against the security of

France, and desertion during time of war. The verdict was handed down by a military court in Clermont-Ferraund.

French Premier Petain had nipped a coup attempt in the bud, by arresting Pierre Lavalle, the Vice Premier and Minister of Foreign Affairs. Lavalle was soon free, however. Hitler, infuriated by Lavalle's arrest, ordered his release. Lavalle was quick to denounce Petain. "Now I know where to find my friends," he announced among Germans. Over the past few weeks, Petain had been holding secret conversations with the British government, assuring them that he would not fight with Hitler against them. At the same time, Lavalle had called openly for closer collaboration with Germany. Lavalle planned to seize Petain during a ceremony in Paris and then set up a new government in Versailles with Germany's support. Petain had learned of the plan and ordered Lavalle arrested.

Meanwhile in the western hemisphere, Leon Trotsky, the most persistent critic of Joseph Stalin, died in Mexico City. He was bludgeoned with an ax at his home in Coyoacan. Stalin was suspected of ordering the murder. Trotsky accused Stalin of masterminding an unsuccessful assassination attempt previously. To the very end, Trotsky spoke of Bolshevism. "I am sure of victory of the fourth international," he whispered on his deathbed. The assassin was a frequent visitor to Trotsky's home and had been variously identified as a Canadian, a journalist, educated in France, and the son of a Belgian diplomat.

1940 slipped into 1941. Hitler continued his conquests, solidifying the occupation of France. Having decided not to invade Britain, Hitler was making dramatic changes in his war policies. He had wanted France and Spain to fight with him. He held separate meetings with French Premier Henri Phillipe Petain, Vice Premier Lavalle, and General Franco. German officials refused to discuss the meeting, but diplomatic sources believed that Hitler wanted to start a new campaign against Britain at Gibraltar and in North Africa. Petain rejected a demand from Hitler that he surrender the French Navy to Germany, but

Hitler insisted he be able to use the French bases on the continent and in Africa. Lavalle, apparently, was more flexible with Hitler than Petain was, and the Fuhrer sensed he might be more open-minded to collaboration. When Hitler met with Franco for the first time, he asked for Spain's help with an assault on Gibraltar. In return, Franco demanded that Hitler replace the wheat and oil that would be cut off by Britain. No such agreement ever took place.

Relations between Russia and Germany, having weakened, were reinforced on November 12, 1940, when Hitler wined and dined Russian Foreign Minister Vyacheslav Molotov in Berlin. Vyacheslav Molotov and Joachim von Ribbentrop had been and remained the chief spokesmen for Germany and Russia throughout all relations between the countries serving directly as immediate underlings and the voices for Hitler and Stalin. Molotov was met by German Foreign Minister Joachim von Ribbentrop at the Berlin train station, without the usual ostentatiousness of a military display so as to downplay the importance of the meeting and moot questions of the Anglo-Russian relations. During a three-hour private meeting, Hitler and Molotov discussed the new political order in Europe and the role Japan might play in the redrawn map of Eurasia. After the meeting, Molotov and the staff dined at a meal feeding 250 people, including 100 high-ranking Nazi officials. Although Russia's relations with other nations were excluded from the talks, both Rome and Nazi Party members expected talks to result in Russia's joining the German/Italian/Japanese Alliance. This was quite a reversal since that pact was forged in October-November 1936 when the Fascist nations agreed to defense against the spread of Communism.

While these negotiations were going on in Germany, President Roosevelt was reelected as the first man in American history to win a third term in the White House. Elected along with him was Vice President Henry A. Wallace, who had been the Secretary of Agriculture. While the vote was much closer than the Roosevelt landslide of 1936, the President handily defeated the Republican candidate Wendell Wilkie. President Roosevelt, addressing a crowd at Hyde Park,

New York, promised to be "the same Franklin Roosevelt you have known." In the fireside chat shortly after his election, heard throughout much of the world, President Roosevelt described the United States as being an arsenal of democracy. While determined to keep America out of war, the President said, "The United States must send more war supplies to those in the front lines of democracy's battle." He said, "No dictator or combination of dictators would halt America's aide to those fighting Nazi Germany." The President ruled out any peace talks "until it was certain that all aggressor nations abandon all thoughts of dominating or conquering the world." "The experience of the past two years," he said, "had proven beyond a doubt that no nation can appease the Nazis." "No man can tame a tiger into a kitten by stroking it." FDR told the American people that his purpose is "To keep you now and your children later and your grandchildren much later, out of war for preservation of American independence." "Not since Jamestown or Plymouth Rock had our American civilization been in such danger as now" he said, adding that "there must be more shipments of guns, planes and ships, more of everything for the Allies."

Africa was in the news as Italian troops unwilling to face the British bayonets at close quarters as the perimeter of their Tobruk defense was cracked had yielded the city to the Allied forces. The British forces had pushed within eight miles of the city and the Italians threw up two lines of defense in the perimeter 30 miles long around the city. Australian troops had crawled out of the trenches and after feints all along the line, followed as tanks forced a gap in the east. The Italians who had trained their guns on the front surrendered by the thousands as the Australians fanned out behind them. Free French and British forces continued sporadic attacks along the line to prevent the Italians from bringing reinforcements to the site on the main assault. The Australians were also assisted by bombing attacks from the British ships and planes off the coast. The Italian government conceded the loss of the vital port city in Libya. Further east, Germany's General Erwin Rommel had arrived in Tripoli with orders from Hitler to reverse the setbacks that the Axis had suffered. The first units of his Afrika Korps had now gone ashore. They were specially trained by Rommel for action in the desert. He was to command two divisions, one of them armored the other motorized.

Italian forces in Libya, which had been under the command of Marshal Rudolpho Gratziani, had been on the run for several weeks since they had lost the city of Tobruk. The British forces had also occupied Benghazi and things in the African theater looked bleak for the Axis. Benito Mussolini was infuriated by the defeats and fired his top generals. It was an entirely different war in Africa than the tragedy of France.

It was with much joy that we in Cleveland, possibly for the first time, began to realize that, in fact, the mighty Axis war machine could be stopped and that it was not invincible. My father had made the assessment that the African campaign would be quite different from the war in France. He had assumed that this was the proving ground of battles which were to come in Europe in years to come. Mark's assessments were accurate and his predictions would come into fruition not too much later. In addition to the optimism we enjoyed in Cleveland about the successful campaign in Africa we now heard that Germany had stabbed its neighbor, Russia, in the back, and invaded that country along a 2,000 mile stretch from the Arctic Region to the Black Sea. Germany and Russia were now in a full scale war as Hitler attempted to fulfill his dream of "lebensraum", or "living space" for the German people.

In a proclamation to the German people, Hitler termed the military attack as the biggest in the history of the world and said Russian and British cooperation threatened the safety of Europe. The action severed the Nazi - Soviet Pact of Non-Aggression signed in 1939.

Could this possibly be the turning point Mark pondered? We had hoped for miracles to stop the Nazi might and thought possibly that this is what we had all been waiting for. The months to come were indeed harrowing as countless thousands of troops were killed on both sides in some of the deadliest battles of all time.

CHAPTER 18

THE WAR YEARS ON THE HOME FRONT

The year of 1941 ended with the Wallach family spread out. My brother had left for the University of Cincinnati, and my sister, Renee, was finishing high-school and would soon depart for the University of Michigan at Ann Arbor. I was still in high school. Athletics was my entire life, i.e., football, baseball, tennis and basketball. Through my teen years, my father continued building homes in Elyria and Lorain, just west of Cleveland, near the steel factories. In view of gasoline rationing and his well-off financial situation, he purchased two new automobiles, a 1941 Chrysler and a 1941 Buick. In this manner, he was able to get more gasoline for his travels. Gasoline had been rationed and one could have an A-Card, B-Card, or C-Card. An A-Card was red and did not allow too much gasoline per week. The B-Cards were green and allowed a little bit more. The C-Card was grey and allowed for the most amount of gasoline. My father somehow managed to get two C-Cards and that gave him all the gasoline he needed enabling him to continue traveling to Elyria and Lorain which were approximately 45 miles from our home. His daily trips involved an extremely hard schedule that he enjoyed most intensely. He worked all day long, overseeing his construction jobs and usually, in the evenings, he could be found in our home library, adding figures, calculating costs to determine new price controls he could use, and figuring out other ways to increase profits. I recall that on several occasions, homes were built that did not show a decent profit and were sold at a loss due to faulty figuring on his part. This was a great aggravation to him, and he concentrated more and more on his book work to see that cost figures were accurately kept. It must be remembered that at that time, there were no such things as calculators to help with calculations, and I remember my father running down long columns of figures to the bottom of the page, all done on paper without electronic aids. In today's modern world, we put the figures into our computers and it calculates the answer for us. This was not the case back in 1941, and my father spent long, tedious and sometimes more or less aggravating days on calculating and figuring his costs out.

The daily schedule at the Wallach house was similar to that of many other families at that time. The total focus was on the radio and the newspaper to see what was happening on the battlefields of Europe. There was much stress as to the differences of opinion as to whether or not the United States should get involved or remain neutral. Much of this country's neutrality had been spent with the backing of England and France by the citizens of this country. The German land-grabbing was not viewed kindly, and it did appear, as the year wound down, that sooner or later, this country, too, would be involved. Much fear was harbored in the hearts of all of us what with Germany's might and its continued conquests of Europe and Russia. What would be next? When would this country be in danger? By the first week of December, 1941, the German forces had advanced to within 20 miles of Moscow, and although they had fallen back under determined Russian counterattacks, the situation there was still quite questionable as to whether Germany might take over Moscow. We felt that if Germany was successful, the United States would soon be involved in the war. Most of my family breathed easier when we learned of the stalwart Russian defense and the Germans being pushed back from Moscow. It was at that time that General Fedor von Bock was daring enough to tell Hitler that no one could reasonably hope to have this operation succeed after the serious loss of the lives of many officers and the tanks being stuck in the mud. Hitler refused to listen to this kind of talk and had already put out announcements that Moscow had fallen or would fall within the next few days. At the same time, almost the same stories could be told of Leningrad and the rest of the Russian front which continued south all the way to the Crimea. Leningrad was under siege, and the Russians fought back ferociously, preventing many of the German troops from joining the assault on Moscow. Listening to the radio and reading the daily newspaper had become an obsession with my family. We could never get enough news of what was happening overseas.

Then all hell exploded on December 7, 1941. Tragically, amid disabled battleships, wounded soldiers, and thousands of unrecognized corpses, Pearl Harbor was aflame in Hawaii after a vicious Japanese attack. The Japanese sank a good part of our fleet. 360 Japanese warplanes had reached the Hawaiian Islands and pulverized the military base at Pearl Harbor where thousands died. Within the month, the U.S. was engaged in a worldwide war. A day after the assault at Pearl Harbor, President Roosevelt said that "America was suddenly and deliberately attacked by the naval and air forces of the empire of Japan. We will gain the inevitable triumph, so help us God." The United States immediately declared war on Japan after the Pearl Harbor attack, with only one dissenting vote in Congress, that of Janet Rankin, the Republican representative from Montana.

Thunderous applause interrupted the President's address to Congress as he remarked that the Japanese onslaught of December 7, 1941, was a date that would "live in infamy." On December 11, American leaders declared war on Japanese Axis Partners Italy and Germany to ensure a world victory of the forces of justice and righteousness over the forces of savagery and barbarism.

What would be next? Would my brother, Benno, be the first member of our family to go to war? Benno by now had turned 18. Conscription was in effect at the time and all able-bodied men over 18 were compelled to serve in the military. Mark and Lena were in a panic at the thought of their eldest son going off to war. Benno was sent off to Detroit to a "Yeshiva," an orthodox Hebrew school that prepared young men to become Rabbis. This was not the type of religion our family practiced, but this was Benno's choice to dodge the draft and avoid military service. My sister, Renee, was enjoying happy days at the University of Michigan at Ann Arbor, having a wonderful time during her college years. I remained at home and played in my high school's football and basketball games.

In the 10th grade, I felt quite fortunate to have been sought by "The Olympians," a fraternal group of 19 high school boys. This group showed great devotion to each other, displaying a camaraderie I had not experienced before or since. It was a true brotherhood with deep and lasting friendships. Being President ot the Olympians during my junior year of high school was the greatest honor I ever had.

We Olympians found our counterparts at the sororities we visited after our own Friday night meetings. The young ladies held meetings similar to ours, and by the time we arrived, had put out the food and drink. We spent the next hour or so "partying" there, and there were many one-on-one relationships.

Romances, of course, often blossomed at the Friday night gatherings. Some progressed into marriage and the subsequent creation of new families. My high-school days in 1943 and 1944 were happy days for me, but my mind was still focused on the information provided by the newspaper as to the war's progression. Our ears were turned toward the radio at every possible opportunity to keep up with what was happening in Europe and the Pacific. My friends and I were young, full of vim, vigor, and vitality, and ready to go and fight. Foolishly, we all looked forward to the day when we, too, would be a part of the armed forces - the Army, the Navy, the Marine Corps, or the Coast Guard - so we could do our part to fight the enemy. Little attention was paid to the fact that once joining the armed forces the possibility of getting killed was very real. My parents worried a great deal about what might happen to their sons. Renee was safe at school and there was no concern that she would be drafted. Benno had switched from the Yeshiva school in Detroit to Hebrew Union College in Cincinnati, where he studied for the Rabbinate. By being so involved in his studies, he was exempt from military service, so at least Mark and Lena's first son would be spared from the war.

Their fear was still present as they knew

of my eagerness to join the military and fight the enemy. In the 11th grade, I spoke of enlisting in the U.S. Navy. My parents were greatly concerned, and they were successful in convincing me that I should at least wait until my 18th birthday. When a young man turned 18, he had to register for the draft within two days of his birthday. Once registered for the draft, the young man waited for his call to recruitment. The youngster never knew if he would be drafted into the army, navy or other branches of the service.

By the time my 18th birthday was in sight, almost all of the draftees I knew had been conscripted into the army. I thought they were pure cannon fodder and I was hell-bent on becoming a sailor in the Navy. Since my birthday was at the end of August, I was not going to wait until that time to be recruited and I enlisted on August 7, 1944. I waited for my call. On August 28, two days after my 18th birthday, I received a letter and phone call instructing me that in two days, I was to report to the downtown post office, ready to go to war. My enthusiasm was dampened by the fears of my parents who saw this whole situation as a horrible nightmare while I saw this as a great opportunity to fight the enemy.

The two days before leaving were difficult ones for all of us. I was soon to leave my parents. Not one day in all of my 18 years had I been away from them and now I was soon to be shipped overseas. On August 30, I reported for my physical examination and was subsequently sent to Great Lakes Naval Training Center, outside of Chicago, where I attended 12 weeks of grueling training.

Mother and Dad were extremely concerned that I would be lost in the war, as so many young men had been killed by this time. The invasion of Normandy in France had occurred just before my recruitment. Thousands of lives were lost there. The American army was now battling the Germans on French soil, and it was only a matter of time before I would be shipped out to partake in war. As I look back, I realize the pain my father experienced as he witnessed his young son leaving home. He dearly loved me and many times over the years, I thought I was really his favorite. I had been gifted with all of his genes and if ever a clone existed between a father and son, this was the situation that existed between my father and me. As for my siblings, my sister, Renee, loved our parents dearly and was greatly loved in return. Benno was an ice-cold fish that no one really understood. He did not share a close relationship with my father or anyone in comparison to what I experienced with my parents. I felt and do to this day feel he is an odd bird totally out of step with the world. This is the best I will say about him, though my feelings run deeper and more in the negative.

Correspondence was important to me during my Navy years. My mother and father were excellent and dutiful writers, often writing me daily. When I had the opportunity, I, too, wrote to them. I had very little time for anything but my very intense training. Recruits had hardly any time for leisure activities such as writing letters. I wrote to my parents whenever possible, as well as to my fraternity brothers and a few girlfriends with whom I felt close. Whatever time was not consumed with training was spent in letter-writing, and I acquired quite a reputation as a correspondent within my company. Never during the war years did my father cease worrying about his youngest son, "Kurtl," a nickname he lovingly gave me. He knew what wars were like, having seen at close quarters and almost firsthand the hardships of World War I during 1914 to 1918. He kept close watch on what was happening throughout the world as every arena was laden with soldiers killing each other. He continued with his construction work and continued to build defense housing as well as luxury homes in our neighborhood of University Heights. This lasted throughout the term of the war.

1944 was an odd and progressive year in many ways. The United States Supreme Court had ruled that "Negroes" could not be barred from voting in the Texas Democratic Primaries. While the decision applied just to Texas, southern members of Congress expressed fear that it could be extended to other southern states as well. Senator James Eastman, the Democrat from Mississippi, said, "It could destroy state sovereignty."

In Syria, rioters with revolvers, axes, and rifles, took to the streets of Damascus, threatened by the idea of seeing women's faces. A fanatical Moslem group hearing rumors of Syrian women removing their veils, organized vocal protests. Their fears were unfounded. The rumors were traced to a young women's culture club, the "Drop of Nook Society". Club members needed a private place to screen a film. They chose the French officer's club which afforded them sufficient space and invited rumors of abandoned veils and wild dancing. With the increasing influence of western ways, many Moslem men feared the emancipation of women. Riots became commonplace. How awful it would be to have women's faces seen.

President Roosevelt in the meantime signed a Bill of Rights granting benefits to veterans of the war. Among the key provisions of this bill was unemployment benefits of $20 per week for up to 52 weeks. I, of course, took advantage of this after my discharge from the Navy a couple of years later, and went on what was then to become known as the 52/20 club and belonged to that through my years in college. In addition, a 50% guarantee of loans up to $2,000 at not more than 4% interest was offered to establish financing for homes or businesses. Grants of $500 a year for four years for training and education plus subsistence payments of $50 to $75 a month were offered. Up to $500 million dollars for additional veterans facilities was a part of this bill as well.

Governor Thomas E. Dewey of New York won the Republican nomination for President, after Governor John W. Bricker of Ohio withdrew from the race. Governor Bricker later won the nomination for Vice President on the first ballot. More than 25,000 Republicans cheered loudly and waved flags and posters greeting their new presidential nominee in Chicago stadium. The Democratic ticket was established as President Roosevelt chose Harry S. Truman to become the Vice Presidential nominee on a ticket on which Roosevelt would seek a fourth term. Senator Truman's nomination on the second ballot was an overwhelming defeat for Vice President Henry A. Wallace's bid for another term. The Vice President had bested Senator Truman on the first ballot but finally was crushed 1,100 to 66 on the second, while Associate Justice William O. Douglas polled just four votes. President Roosevelt had said he would be pleased to have either Truman or Douglas as a running mate. Truman, who rose from relative obscurity in his home state of Missouri was sitting on the platform eating a sandwich when the results of the balloting were announced. Dragged to the microphone by fellow senators, the new nominee seemed a bit stunned by his victory, making a brief, halting speech thanking the delegates at the Chicago convention and vowing to continue the efforts to shorten the war. It was the shortest speech made that day.

The radio brought us news that Glen Miller, the famed orchestra leader was missing. A plane carrying him and two companions disappeared en route from England to France during a U.S.O. trip. The pilot raised no distress call and no wreckage had been spotted by British planes in the area. A master of swing, Miller took his place alongside Duke Ellington, Benny Goodman, Artie Shaw, Tommy and Jimmy Dorsey and

Count Basie. One of the finest band leaders of the era, Miller played the trombone and arranged his orchestra's smooth, satisfying compositions. He was riding the crest of his fame. His song "In the Mood" soared over the airwaves nationally, daily. The Iowa-born band leader was only 40 years old. As teenagers we mourned him as though he were one of our own, a member of the family, yet we hoped in our hearts that maybe one day he would be found. This was not the case and Glen Miller appears to have disappeared from this world forever, as I write this.

CHAPTER 19

WAR AND DISASTER

Although the war for the United States started out disastrously considering Pearl Harbor and the European situation between 1939 and 1942, it now appeared by 1944 that the United States, England, free France, and their allies would eventually be victorious. Allied forces had landed in North Africa in 1942, and the war in that region was won by the Allies later that year. The British routed Nazi Field Marshal Erwin Rommel's Afrika Corps. after giving it a sound thrashing at El Alamein. The Germans and Italians were totally defeated there and headed toward Tobruk where, once again, they were defeated by General Bernard Montgomery's forces who captured some 30,000 men including Ritter von Tho, a commander of the Afrika Corps.

Hundreds of German tanks were destroyed and countless German airplanes were shot down as victory in North Africa set the stage for the invasion of the underbelly of Europe, namely Greece and Italy. Field Marshal Rommel did not have much time to take a breather after his disastrous defeats at El Alamein, Tobruk, and Benghazi. The Desert Fox was cut off from his rear guard by the British column and eventually it was all over there.

In the meantime in the United States, a group of physicists led by Enrico Fermi had achieved the first controlled nuclear chain reaction, opening the way to creation of the atomic bomb and nuclear energy. The scientists built a nuclear powder composed of uranium and graphite on the squash courts of the University of Chicago. The crucial moment had come at 3:45 p.m. on December 1, 1943, when the removal of control rods showed that neutrons from fissuring uranium atoms split other atoms to keep the chain reaction going. The atomic powder was part of the secret Manhattan Project to build an atomic bomb. Germany, at the time, was said to have begun similar efforts and were only a few months behind in their research.

Early in 1943, the largest tank battle of the war had taken place. The Soviets had retaken Kursk one year and three months after it fell to the Nazis. This Russian city of 120,000 people was a vital railroad junction where the Moscow Crimea and the Voronezh-Kiev Lines meet. This was also an essential link in the chain of German outposts in the Ukraine. That summer, the Nazis had held a series of cities stretching south from Kursk several hundred miles to the sea of Azov. They controlled thousands of acres between the Dnieper and the Don. In this area, they launched attacks at Stalingrad and parts of the Caucasus. With Kursk freed, the Soviets hoped to liberate nearby Kharkiv which they were able to do shortly. Their next target was to be Rostov, the southernmost city of the Nazi line, which the Soviets successfully took back.

The war went well for the Allies on all fronts in 1944. The United States vented its power, backing up the British who were stretched to their limit by the relentless Nazi bombings of their country. The Royal Air Force was beginning to fight back and was joined by American bombers and fighters which had switched the emphasis from defense of England to offensive attacks on the continent. The RAF dropped thousands of tons of bombs on Berlin and 1,500 to 2,000 American planes flew over Hamburg, Cologne, Berlin, Koblentz, and Weisbaden almost daily. Millions of lives were lost. The bombings were the most destructive force that the world had ever known.

The Russian battles weakened the German Army sufficiently to allow the Allied victories in Africa and Italy. The subsequent full invasion of the continent on June 6, 1944 became known as D-Day. The war raged on both east and west fronts during 1944-45. It became obvious that Hitler chewed off more than he could handle as Germany began losing battles in both the east and west.

In 1944, Klaus von Stauffenberg and some associates attempted to murder Adolph Hitler on July 20, in the eastern headquarters in Prussia in what was called the "Wolf's

Lair." The Wolf's Lair was Hitler's retreat, similar to the U.S. President's retreat at Camp David. By July of 1944, many high-ranking German officers were convinced that the war was lost. They wanted Hitler to declare an armistice because they felt that Germany would be destroyed by American and English bombings if no such armistice could be attained. Hitler refused any offers of peace. Von Stauffenberg and his group felt the only way to save Germany was to assassinate Hitler. Klaus von Stauffenberg, a high-ranking Nazi officer, placed a bomb in a briefcase underneath the table where Hitler sat. Shortly before the bomb was scheduled to explode, someone moved the briefcase to the other end of the table. It exploded, killing a few officials, but not Hitler. Hitler suffered an injury to his right arm but escaped anything more serious.

Massive trials were held after this assassination attempt, and over 5,000 Germans were tried in court and assassinated by hanging and other forms of military execution. Klaus von Stauffenberg was among those killed. Erwin Rommel, Germany's "Desert Fox" who fought the British in Africa and was considered a great leader in the war, was also executed in Hitler's sweep. Two soldiers were dispatched to Rommel's home where he was recovering from injuries received in a recent battle and told him he could either poison himself and commit suicide or see his entire family killed and then be executed himself. Rommel decided to take the poison pills. He was given a military funeral with much pomp and fanfare.

The winter of 1944 saw the Russians demolishing the German Army as it retreated west back toward Germany. The Allied invasion of France on June 6 and the Battles on the Western front against the American and English Armies drove the German Army back into Germany. Germany's fate was sealed on all fronts, with the Allied and Russian Armies victories. On May 8, 1945, Germany capitulated and V-E Day was celebrated (Victory in Europe). Hitler committed suicide in his bunker in Berlin a few days earlier with Eva Braun, the woman he married hours before their double suicide.

Eva Braun the photographer's assistant with whom he had become infatuated, was brought by Hitler to Berchtesgaden, his mountaintop retreat as his great crisis grew. He was extremely sensitive to remarks made about Eva at this time , and it was said that people would wind up in concentration camps if they said anything about her, complimentary or otherwise. She was Hitler's playmate and pet becoming his wife only hours before they both committed suicide. After their deaths, the Nazis appointed Karl Doenitz to succeed Hitler. He and Alfred Jodl eventually signed the capitulation papers as Germany surrendered. Doenitz and Jodl were later sentenced to death for war crimes but were not then executed. Doenitz was sent to Spandau prison from which he was released in 1956. Jodl was hanged in 1946.

Back in the United States, I had volunteered for the attack boat squadron of the underwater demolition teams and was training in Fort Pierce, Florida. I lied to my mother and father, telling them that the U.S.A.T.B. stood for "United States Air Training Base" whereas it was in reality, the "U.S.

Amphibious Training Base." My mother and father were extremely concerned about me upon finding out the truth that I had volunteered for the "amphibs" and now was in grave danger for my life. I had scared them to a point that could not easily be described. It was in late 1944 that they found out that this training was created for the boys who would invade the islands in the Pacific in the war against Japan. The amphibious forces were the ones that hit the beaches and brought the soldiers and Marines on to land. They were the first in and usually among the first casualties. Underwater Demolition Teams and attack boats were, in fact, expendable, as a great number of these boys were lost during the first two days of every invasion. Saipan, Guadalcanal, the Solomons, and the Gilbert Islands were all examples of amphib heroics as was the June 6 invasion at Normandy where so many thousands died.

My parents saw the danger of what was to come and found out that I was indeed in the attack boat training program. They were more concerned than ever and came to Florida to see me off for what might be the last time they would ever see me. My father and mother greeted me at Fort Pierce, Florida on December 7, 1944 and stayed in a hotel in Vero Beach, some 15 miles north of Fort Pierce. They had somehow gotten through to one of the commanders of the base, and some special privileges were given to me. I was able to come into town occasionally and be with my parents during the two-week period they were there. They were greatly fearful that this was the last time they would see me alive. I, too, was afraid, for the percentage of lives lost in the attack boats and underwater demolition teams was extremely high. It was a very difficult time for all of us.

After their tearful visit, they returned to Cleveland as empty nesters. Their oldest son was in school, Renee was at the University of Michigan, and I, of course, was about to go to a war to hit the beaches on a far off island in the Pacific Theater of the war. It was a difficult time for my father, particularly in view of his pessimistic analysis of the situation. He had felt that though the war was going well, there could still be many hundreds of thousands of lives lost before the disaster of

Mark, Lena and Kurt in Vero Beach, Florida 1944

World War II was over. When that would be, Lord only knew, he said. His youngest son being in the midst of the war gave him great heartache. This is difficult to describe. I had promised I would send a letter daily, if such a promise could be kept. Of course, this was not possible as leisure time was rarely available.

Kurt becoming a casualty of war or even participating in the fighting as amphibious forces hit the beaches in the Pacific never became a reality. After shipping out of Ft. Pierce I was sent to Mobile, Alabama for several days and then on to Algiers Naval Base near New Orleans.

At Algiers we were introduced to the LST 1040. We boarded and got rather well acquainted with what this ship was like. We came to the conclusion finally that it would sail the oceans as a flea in a bathtub. The assessment was rather correct since the ship had a round bottom, very little speed and maneuverability which could be measured from zero to none. We stayed on the 1040 for a few days and I made friends with a young chap by the name of Anthony Anderra who, shortly after our acquaintance, became quite ill, likely pneumonia, after we set out to sea. Tony remained in his bunk for days on end and appeared to be getting no better as time went on. There was no doctor aboard to care for him and with great regret one day we noticed that Tony was no longer moving and had, in fact, died in his sleep. Tony was 18 years old, like the rest of us. There was hardly a young sailor aboard not in a state of shock as this was the first envisioned wartime tragedy that we had experienced. It was a real eye opener into the reality of life. We had Tony's body aboard until we pulled into Panama where it was delivered to the hospital to be sent back to the United States. We heard no more about him, nor from his family. From Panama we traveled on west to an island in the Solomons where we sat and waited what appeared to be a lifetime. Something big was happening yet none of us knew what it was.

The desolate island was thickly overgrown from shore to shore except for an airstrip which ran across the center of it. Some P-51's and P-47's took off from there almost daily, but otherwise it was uneventful, except for the fact that there were many thousand soldiers and marines bivouacked and apparently poised for whatever was to be. There was a considerable amount of mechanized equipment including trucks, amphibious ducks, tanks, and construction vehicles, along with close to 100 jeeps on the island. Something big was going on. What it was, we did not know but we shared the thought that it could not be too far in the distance, since everything was ready, ready, ready, ready and the men of the army, construction corps and marines were totally prepared.

While sitting on a bunk one evening, I was called in to the Lieutenant's quarters and was advised that the interpreter's job for which I had applied months earlier in Fort Pierce, Florida, was being considered and that I would be shipped back to the United States. Within 48 hours I was on a plane headed for Washington which would soon land in Panama. Upon arriving at France Field on the isthmus I was told that orders had been changed and that I was to be shipped back. I requested a liberty in the city of Colon where I promptly overstayed my time off. A.W.O.L. (Absent Without Official Leave) was a bit more desirable than what I saw happening in the Solomons from where I knew we would be shipped on to an invasion within days. I stayed A.W.O.L. for a few days and upon reading in the paper that the American forces had hit the island of Okinawa I came back to France Field, reporting in that I had gotten drunk, had been lost and could not find my way back. This was a story which, of course, was not to be believed and a short period of time in the brig was suffered after a "captain's mast" (a low form of court martial).

After this unhappy incident I was sent down to the submarine base of Coco Solo where I spent the next 18 months. Although Coco Solo was never a pleasure, it afforded me "life." I was to be safe for the remainder of the war, staying put there for the duration plus a year.

As things turned out, my first visit to the brig in early March of 1945 was not to be my last. The city of Colon, several miles from

Coco Solo, had become our watering hole and we had the privilege of going into town minimally two or three times a week. Colon-Cristobal is a very old Spanish community where the Panama Canal enters into the bay which connected directly to the Atlantic Ocean. Colon-Cristobal was the place where many soldiers, sailors and marines had their first feel of land, many times after weeks out at sea.

All the ships coming from the Pacific theater of war and heading toward their destinations on the Atlantic coast of the United States came through the Panama Canal. Ships that had been at sea for several weeks at a time without seeing port pulled in almost daily. At times there was total bedlam in town as countless thousands of men invaded the city. The men of the services landed there oftentimes after trips from Europe or patrolling the Atlantic Ocean. Since, for the most part, liquor was not allowed aboard ship (except for officer's quarters) the young warriors often turned wild as soon as they hit Colon-Cristobal, twin cities which had been transformed into a great den of iniquity with bars, photo studios, whorehouses and the like, being the main trade and the backbone of commerce. Streets such as "D

Street, or Cash Street" were specifically reserved for the servicemen. In fact, they were out of bounds for civilians. The primary commerce on Cash Street and D Street was houses of ill repute which were on both sides of the streets for close to a mile. Activity here was wild and seldom was it quiet. It was said that at least 20 to 25% of the patients at the hospitals came from Cash Street and D Street and it was indeed a rare day that there were not at least three or four fights up and down the streets. Most of these could likely be attributed to the fact that these young boys were unable to hold their liquor and that they had been totally out of touch for so long. It cannot be said that the "ladies of the night" did not play a part in causing much of the mayhem. There were many times that, thinking the customer to be too drunk to know the difference, the girls would "liberate" the customer's wallet. This, in turn, as often as not, set the young warrior on to the prostitute sending her to the hospital. At times, the situation was reversed. Cash Street, in particular, during the war would become an epic which could be written into the annals of Panamanian history. Not only once, but on several occasions was I too, involved in some of the melees of Cash Street and D Street. The city was marked with "pro stations." These were areas of approximately 1,000 square feet which we were instructed to visit and take medication onto and into our genitals to protect us from possible social diseases after we had intercourse with the prostitutes.

There was very little venereal disease in Colon or in Cristobal due to the fact that the authorities were extremely careful, not only that the service men were to go to the "pro stations" (this was mandated), but the girls who inhabited Cash Street and D Street were inspected physically by military doctors from the bases. In fact, they were clean. Panama and the United States had a contract where the United States government guaranteed a certain amount of jobs to Panamanian citizens. In order to comply with the contract, the various bases on the isthmus employed much local labor, thus making it easier for the Navy and the Army personnel, who did less heavy physical labor than would otherwise have been needed. In addition, the prostitutes having been inspected by the doctors (military) were also considered to be employees of the United States government. In Balboa and Panama City as well as Colon and Cristobal there were several hundred prostitutes who were on the American payroll via the servicemen.

After I was at Coco Solo for a while, I had finally come to the conclusion that it would be wisest to stay out of town when the "fleet was in". It was during these times that there might be anywhere from 3,000 to 10,000 sailors, soldiers or marines descending onto the city, which almost assured drunken brawls and mayhem. My smartest decision was not to be there and it became my practice to stay on the base during these times.

For the most part, time in Panama, for me, was reasonably peaceful with several exceptions. Liberty in town, being one of these. A foolish "incident" caused me to have my second visit to the brig in early 1945. It was on one of these visits into town that my friend, Eddie Rijinsky, had a few too many and it was only due to my help that I was able to get him back and into the barracks. Eddie was a fine fellow but when drunk was not only incorrigible, but totally uncontrollable. Upon coming back to our bunks after 10 p.m., he thought it might be a great idea to turn some of the double decker bunks over as other sailors were asleep. My battling him in hopes of containing him and preventing him from doing this, finally became a losing proposition, as he turned over two bunks and caused a small riot, to which our Chief Petty Officer, Mike Hunt, was called. Mike was a no nonsense chief. He came in with his flashlight and the first thing he did upon seeing what was going on, was to smash Eddie across the head with it, opening a big gash. I lost control at seeing this happening and landed a haymaker on the Chief's nose, which I believe broke it. He and I battled for a minute before I was restrained and put under arrest. Within days I was ready for my second "Captain's Mast." The commander in charge of the Captain's Mast saw fit to put me in the marine brig for three days on bread and water. My incarceration started on April 11, 1945. I had now been a veteran of my second incarceration in the brig and did not find it too difficult, although, when the marines had me crawling on the concrete floor without pants on for three hours one night, the agony of the blood which oozed from my knees was not much enjoyed.

My departure from the brig was on April 14th and upon strolling back onto the base, I noticed the flags at half mast. I believe I must have asked at least three men why the flags were at half mast before one answered me telling me that I was some sort of a dumb jackass not to know that President Roosevelt had died. It was two days after his death, and everyone throughout the world mourned.

CHAPTER 20

THE AGONY AND CALAMITIES

The war continued better and better for American forces as they were successful in retaking island after island in the Pacific. The Russians were winning their war on the Eastern Front and various American and British invasions of the continent on the west followed the Normandy invasion. The Nazis had begun a new reign of terror against the Hungarian Jews as they tried to fortify the country against the coming Russian attack on the homeland. Shortly after their invasion of Hungary in 1944, the Germans began rounding up all Jews and dispatching them to the gas chambers at Auschwitz. The man in charge of the roundup was Adolph Eichmann, who told the Jewish Council in Budapest, "You don't know who I am. I am a butcher. I am thirsty for blood." The end of the war saw Eichmann being sought by Jewish agents for years and their attempt to bring him to justice. In 1961 he was finally found in Argentina and clandestinely pulled out of the country and flown to Israel for trial. Though Eichmann received a fair trial in Israel, it was obvious from first statements of the prosecution that a solid case had been built against him and that there was no escaping for him, of the truth and the realities of his deeds. The trial ended with a decision that Adolph Eichmann should be hung after he was convicted of crimes against humanity. He was finally put on the gallows and hung until dead in 1962.

A Hungarian official said Hitler executed a classic stab in the back to invade Hungary in early 1944. He summoned Hungarian leaders, presumably to discuss the withdrawal of the troops from Russia to increase defenses back home. As soon as the Hungarian dictator, Nicholas von Horthy arrived, Hitler had him arrested and the invasion of Hungary began. Hitler's invasion of Hungary was a desperate move. Ten of his divisions were bottled up in the Ukraine in Bessarabia. The Russians' next targets were Poland, Romania, and Hungary. My father was in mourning for his brothers, sisters-in-law, nephews, and nieces who had all been killed in the Ukraine by the Nazis. The Germans killed and tortured mercilessly throughout the countries they invaded. As the war dragged on, it became evident that it was only a matter of time before the Thousand Year German Empire as declared by Adolph Hitler would fall. Allied planes were bombarding Stuttgart, Dresden, Berlin and Leipzig from the west and the Soviets were moving their armed forces coming from the east. The campaign in France went well as Belgium, Holland, Luxemburg, and most of France were soon liberated.

On February 14, 1945, Dresden, known as the "Florence of Germany," became a molten, blazing mass. Allied bombs rained on the city continuously for two days. Priceless art work and architecture from the 17th and 18th centuries were destroyed. More than 100,000 people, most of them civilians, were killed. Throughout the war, the Allies kept a respectable distance from Dresden. It was not an industrial town, but an historic residential city. Many of the buildings were rare examples of Rococco and Baroque styles. Several museums housed paintings by Italian, Dutch, and Flemish masters. Respect for this cultured city had now vanished as 245 R.A.F. Lancaster bombers battered Dresden with incendiaries and 2 ton bombs. At noon the following day, U.S. B-17's pummeled the city. That evening, the R.A.F. with 550 bombers returned. The city could hardly defend itself as it was never equipped to withstand that kind of firepower. Approximately eight or nine bombers were downed by German aircraft. Why was Dresden attacked? The Soviets had assisted in weakening the German defenses in the area. British Air Marshal Arthur Harris had supported an offense on the city. Yet, there was an outcry from many of the Allied nations. If we had bombed Dresden, what was to prevent the Luftwaffe from destroying Oxford or other treasured Allied cities? The deadliest bombing of all time fell on statues, paintings, and ancient churches. These treasures belonged to us all, it was said. Nevertheless, it was a revenge tactic and was carried out with a vengeance.

At the same time, American forces were victorious in the Pacific. After four days of fighting, the Marine platoon finally succeeded in reaching the top of Mt. Surabachi on the southernmost tip of Iwo Jima and raised the American flag in triumph. Conquest of the heavily fortified mountain had been one of the first objectives of the invasion of this most strategic island located only 750 miles south of Tokyo. The task of neutralizing the defenses and scaling the mountains had fallen to the men of the 28th Regiment of the 5th Marine Division. When Navy Secretary James Forestall saw the American flag from the beachhead, he told Lieutenant General Holland M. Smith that the raising of the American flag on Surabachi beach means the presence of the Marine Corps for the next 500 years.

In March of 1945, Anne Frank, the little Dutch girl who had written a diary that would become famous throughout the world, died in the concentration camp at Bergen-Belsen. Half-starved and unconscious from fever, she rolled off her bunk and fell lifeless to the floor. She was only 14 years old. Anne Frank had kept a most remarkable diary while she hid with her family in the attic of a house in Amsterdam for over a year. She recorded all of her feelings - fear over being captured by the Nazis, and joy of her budding sexuality was beautifully recorded in her book. One of her last entries described her conviction that all people are basically good.

The war was soon to end, and the horrors of the Nazi death camps were finally to be made known to the American public and the world. As American troops freed the camp at Buchenwald in April 1945, they were greeted by the dead, or so it seemed. Slave laborers lying on their bare bunks could barely raise their heads to see their liberators. Their muscles were eaten away. Maggots settled in the corners of their sunken eyes as they watched the G.I.'s tread silently by. Some of the soldiers were filled with superstition, recalling warnings to step softly over graves as they walked where over 50,000 innocent people had met their deaths. Buchenwald was founded by the Nazi party in 1933. At that time, the camp had mostly dispensed with "Juden," the German-Jews. The Nazi enemy list grew, however, with the development of the war. The 20,000 prisoners found alive on April 12 included Poles, Hungarians, French, Russians, Dutch, Belgians, Yugoslavians, Austrians, Italians, and even Spaniards who had opposed Franco, as well as other nationalities.

A committee formed by the liberating American Army assessed conditions at Buchenwald for Allied headquarters. They described the prisoners as the intelligentsia and the leadership personnel from throughout Europe. Among the inmates were four anti-Vichy members of the French Parliament. The report went on to say that anyone of outstanding intellectual and moral qualifications, democratic or anti-Nazi inclination as well as their relatives were systematically murdered at the camp. Both Jew and Christian were treated cruelly, although Jews were given much worse treatment than others. Typically, prisoners were kept for six weeks during which time their food intake was restricted. They were expected to lose 40% of their body weight. During that time, prisoners never received Red Cross packages. S.S. personnel appropriated them for themselves. Inmates served as laborers and were subject to random beatings and torture. Some were guinea pigs in testing the effects of lethal germs, amputations, toxins, and suspected antitoxins. Few survived these experiments. Some S.S. personnel kept the flesh of victims. These bits of skin, burned with tattoos, were prized possessions.

Most of those who lived through the six-week period were led to the gas chambers and suffocated. The bodies were transported to one of the six incinerators there. Each furnace could burn three bodies at a time, in about 20 minutes. The corpses were fully reduced to ashes, destroying all evidence of the hardship and torture experienced at the hands of the Nazis. The incinerators ran out of coal for a ten day period in March. According to the witnesses, bodies were stacked in the camp like firewood. Eventually, 1,800 corpses lay outside the barracks. A fatigued detail of laborers was rounded up and made to haul the bodies into trucks. They accompanied the trucks out of the camps to a nearby woods. The detail dug a large burial pit, dragged the bodies into the pit, refilled it with earth, and followed their instructions to leave one end of the pit empty. The S.S. guards then shot each member of the fatigued detail and cast them into the empty part of the mass grave.

Some of the German prison guards lived in their hometowns with their families and among neighbors. They witnessed the passing of the days from sunrise to sunset. Their wives and mothers fondly called them to the dinner table, and they ate with relish. Their hunger suggests something moved inside them, something inhales and exhales, yet somewhere in the recesses of their minds, they knew their acts at Buchenwald rendered them separate and apart from humanity. In my mind they were already dead for the rest of their lives.

By April 1945, as the war was winding down in Europe, the news of Hitler's atrocities spread through the United States. Hitler had committed suicide and the country's attention now focused on Japan. Mark grew worried for his son. He knew the islands close to the Japanese shore had to be taken and feared that Kurt might be detached from Panama and sent to the Pacific. Fortunately, my father's fears were not realized. The atomic bomb was dropped on Hiroshima and Nagasaki during the first week of August in 1945. The United States gave peace a tumultuous welcome a few days thereafter. The long awaited V-J Day (Victory over Japan) had come and the war ended. In New York City, people spontaneously danced in the streets. In San Diego, drunken sailors broke shop windows; on highways in the mid-west, staid and somber farmers honked their car horns as if they were delinquent teenagers. In Italy, the Andrew Sisters sang "Don't Sit Under the Apple Tree" to U.S. troops. Maxine announced the news of Japan's surrender that meant the end of the war as she read from a slip of paper someone handed to her. There was instant silence. After a moment, hats and shoes volleyed into the air. When the boys came home, they may have found the girls to have changed. They began working alongside "Rosie the Riveter" in factories and plants, developing a new sense of self-reliance in women. But the letters they received from their girls said come home, "Let's make the kind of home our parents had."

The German empire crumbled. Hitler was gone and left only tragic memories. Kurt Wallach still found himself in Colon, Panama, where he spent over a year and a half, much to the great joy of his father who had so feared for Kurt's life. Panama was a safe haven for him and his father relished every day that he knew that I was there. Though the duty was hard, with such assignments as hanging over the side of ships in 105 degree weather and scraping rust for 8 to 10 hours a day. It was a safe place and the fear of losing Kurt on the beaches of some far-off land was no longer present.

In Japan, Emperor Hirohito addressed his nation over the radio. Citizens had not been allowed to hear his voice before. He did not use the word "surrender" in his address, but the people knew the cease-fire was on Allied terms. They knew their lives were irrevocably changed. The atomic bombs dropped on Hiroshima and Nagasaki and the Soviet Union's invasion of Manchuria had indeed forced Japan to her knees. Japan agreed to modified terms of the Potsdam conference as allied forces were to occupy the nation and enforce demilitarization. Europe had less reason to celebrate than the United States. Warsaw, Berlin, Paris, and London had all crumbled under a six-year assault. Starvation haunted Europe, Asia, and Africa. "Let us never forget the 50 million who died" became a common household phrase.

The war was over but President Franklin Delano Roosevelt, who died on April 12, 1945, never had the pleasure of seeing it end. The unexpected death of the 31st President in his clapboard cottage in Warm Springs, Georgia, had stunned the nation and the world. An attending doctor said, "the 63 year old President died of a cerebral hemorrhage." The President had been in Warm Springs since the end of March resting up from the rigors of trying to bring an end to the war. His death came at a time of high triumph for the armies and fleets under his command as armies and fleets were at the gates of Berlin and at the shores of Japan's home island and gathering to frame a United Nations charter to assure world peace.

Only hours before his death, President

Roosevelt had been posing for a portrait by Elizabeth Shumatoff commissioned by his long-time friend, Lucy Mercer. In the early afternoon, the President murmured, "I have a terrible headache." He died a short time later and his death was announced by the White House that afternoon. Less than two hours later, Vice President Harry Truman was sworn in as President of the United States.

While President Roosevelt had appeared in declining health in prior months, the rest at Warm Springs seemed to have restored some of his vigorous health. No members of his family were with him at the end. Mrs. Roosevelt had been attending a Washington meeting of the Thrift Club when told to return to the White House. There she was told of her husband's death. She sent messages to their sons, all of them in the services, by saying, "He did his job as he would want you to do. Bless you all, and all our love. Mother."

The White House flag was lowered to half staff, the first time marking the death of an occupant since Warren Harding died in 1923. As the news of Roosevelt's death spread throughout the city, tearful men and women gathered outside the White House and across the street in the square. President Roosevelt, a New Yorker who was educated at Groton, Harvard and Columbia, was considered one of the most remarkable men ever to occupy the White House. He was responsible for initiating the New Deal, the activist federal effort to bring the nation out of the deep depression after his election in 1932. He was re-elected in a landslide in 1936 and in a break with tradition he sought and won an unprecedented third term in 1940, as well as a fourth term in 1944. His impact on the nation and the war was perhaps expressed best in the tribute on the Senate floor by Senator Robert A. Taft, the Ohio Republican and frequent political adversary who termed him, "The greatest figure of our time." "One who died a hero of the war for he literally worked himself to death in the service of the American people."

Funeral services were held later that week in the East Room of the White House with only high officials attending since the chamber was able to accommodate only 200 people. The body then was taken to the late president's home town of Hyde Park, New York, where he was buried in a plot near the Roosevelt home.

It was not more than three weeks later that the maniacal tyrant behind the force of the European war was dead. Adolph Hitler, desperate and bitter, smelling Germany's demise, had committed suicide in Berlin.

In the light of history, Hitler may have been seen as a demented yet determined tyrant. At the height of his unparalleled political career he seemed invincible. He had vanquished nine nations, repulsed Europe's greatest power, devised an economic and social fabric based on the deadly subjugation of millions and hypnotically imposed his will on millions more. Over 65 million Germans glorified this demagogue as the savior of Deutschland. In the end he forced them into the abyss of a nightmarish hell, while Franklin Delano Roosevelt had become the president of a desperate nation, in shock. Its citizens had lost hope, barely survived, in despair and had little confidence for attaining not only a good but even a mere livable existence where the basic needs could be readily attained. Their powers grew and ebbed as they both struggled to achieve during the same years of history. Hitler would be remembered as the beast, the villain and the most evil force the world had ever known, while Roosevelt would be remembered as the hero, redeemer and the knight in shining armor. Any parallel in their reign could only be drafted through chronology, yet this chronology must indeed be seen by future historians as one of the most unusual coincidences of history.

CHAPTER 21

NOW IT IS OVER

By 1946 the war was over. Many items of interest appeared in the papers daily that were not of the ominous and fearful variety to which we had become accustomed throughout the war. We no longer heard of so many thousands dying here and there. Instead, history was now being written with such interesting items as France's Marshal Henri Petain having been found guilty of collaborating with the enemy. He had received a death sentence although he was 89 years old. His death sentence was eventually commuted before he died a natural death. Petain was to be remembered as the savior of Verdun in World War I. His change of character and turn of events was difficult for many French people to comprehend.

Korea was partitioned into two countries,

with the 38th parallel dividing North Korea and South Korea. General Hideki Tojo, the Premier of Japan at the time of the Pearl Harbor attack, was arrested as a war criminal along with other members of his general staff and attempted suicide by trying to shoot himself. American doctors treated him and saved him from dying by his own hand only to see him be executed for his war crimes.

A short time later two prominent Nazi collaborators, Pierre Lavalle of France and Vidkun Abraham Quisling of Norway were executed for aiding German occupation of their countries. Lavalle, who had served as Premier of the Vichy government during the German occupation of France, was shot by a firing squad. With his last breath, he shouted, "Vive la France." Lavalle, too, had attempted suicide before his execution by consuming a vial of poison that he had concealed on his person for more than a year. Quisling, who served as the head of the State Council of Norway during the five years of German occupation, had been convicted of high treason. He was 58 years old when he was sentenced to death for aiding the German invasion of Norway and deserting from the Norwegian Army, causing the death of many thousands of Norwegians including well over 1,000 Jews who were deported to Germany. He was also convicted of accepting money from the Nazis. He was indeed a traitor of the worst kind, both to his country and his countrymen and women.

Old "Blood and Guts," America's most cantankerous war hero, General George S. Patton, was injured in an automobile accident later in the year. The resulting chest wounds gave way to fatal lung congestion and he died, but not in battle, at the age of 60.

Charles DeGaulle, who was elected President of the French Provincial Government, marched triumphantly under the Arch d'Triumph after Paris was liberated from the Germans. His election came four years after DeGaulle fled a defeated country. He declared from England that he was the head of Free France. Henri Petain, whose Vichy government condemned DeGaulle to death in 1940, had just received his own death sentence.

Back on the home front, the first black ballplayer was signed by a baseball team in the National League. Jack Roosevelt Robinson, the Georgia-born player from the Kansas City Monarchs Negro League, joined the Brooklyn Dodgers. The Dodgers' spokesperson said Robinson's signing was not to be interpreted as a gesture to solving racial problems. He said that Robinson, son of sharecropper and grandson of a slave, was a four sports star at the University of Los Angeles and became an All American as a halfback. The signing was achieved by Branch Ricky, President and part-owner of the Dodgers, who hoped to see the 26-year old shortstop playing at Ebbets Field in Brooklyn. This happened soon thereafter.

I was still in Panama and was to remain there for some time to come. Finally, finally, finally, on August 7, 1946, Kurt was discharged from the Navy and returned to the United States, first landing in Miami, Florida then on to Los Angeles, California to spend two weeks with a girlfriend, Tami, then arriving back home in Cleveland, Ohio at the end of August where the arrival was cheered by the family. Life for my father, was happy, now that the war was over and his youngest son was home and safe.

My sister had met Harvey Harris at school and married him in November 1946. Harvey was a veteran who had fought in the Battle of the Bulge and turned out to be a wonderful brother-in-law and a great son-in-law to my parents. Harvey and Renee gave my parents two grandchildren who became the joy of their lives. The entire family loved him from the day he became known to us.

My father was ready to assist any of us financially whenever we needed help. My brother, Benno, seemed always to have some financial wants, and Mark him helped quite a bit after he had left Cleveland. He was constantly in need and I felt, and still do, that he was and is what we would call an "unglück." Renee did not need any assistance getting started in her marriage. Her husband, Harvey, worked hard and always made a living. They lived only a few blocks from my parents in Shaker Heights, with their two daughters, Judith and Pamela. They were a joy to my parents.

Kurt had never been a financial burden on his father and was intent on earning his own way wherever he could. After graduating from Western Reserve University in 1949, I continued my studies under the G.I. Bill of Rights, and went on toward a Master's Degree in Speech and Hearing Pathology. I did not receive my M.A.; business activity took precedence and I did not finish my thesis although all courses were satisfactorily completed. While in college, I started a business retailing storm windows and storm doors. This became a very profitable venture. Harvey, my brother-in-law, and I were partners with Harvey at first the senior partner. Later, he went into the business of building single family homes, leaving the entire business to me. The company prospered and I sold the window business at an excellent profit in 1956.

Were it not for a great desire on my part to move my family to Florida and enjoy the year round summer, we would have remained in this industry for unforeseen years to come. In the long run, the decision turned out to be a very good one as my small family found total happiness after moving to Miami, Florida. Mark and Lena greatly regretted the move, since a very unpleasant separation resulted. My father, Mark, had spent many hours attempting to convince me to remain in Cleveland. It was to no avail as Florida was to become our future home. Though missing the family very much, the decision was never regretted. Mother and dad became very frequent visitors to the "sunny south" in the winters and although we missed each other very much during the year, the winter visits were savored and we made the most of them spending many leisure hours together.

CHAPTER 22

THE POST WAR YEARS

There was always a lot of rivalry among my mother's sisters. Many arguments took place among Jetty, Elsie, Regie, and Lena. These arguments were endless and one disagreement perpetuated the next. My father, many times, was involved to a degree, and his relationships with his sisters-in-law were not good. My father's family was quite the opposite. He had warm, loving relationships with his two brothers, Joseph and A.T., and their families. What a shame, I thought, that Mother and her sisters couldn't get along like Dad did with his brothers.

A.T. came to the United States in 1900 and after opening a business he married Pauline Fell. (Unfortunately, Pauline died at a young age during the 1920's.) Their son, Edward, a Harvard graduate and wrestler on Harvard's wrestling team, became an attorney. As a graduation gift, A.T. sent him on a trip to Magdeburg to visit my family there in 1927. Edward went to Chorostkow to meet his father's brothers and their families. A.T.'s daughter, Claire, was born in 1933, after he married Florence Benedict, his second wife. Edward, in turn, married Dorothy and they had two children, a son, David, and a daughter, Paula. Joseph, my father's older brother, had a first marriage that ended in divorce. He and his first wife had a son they named Billy. He and his second wife, Marguerite, had a daughter, Caroline.

Everyone loved my father. He was honest to a fault, trustworthy, and a genuinely nice human being. His word was his bond, and he was probably one of the hardest working men one would ever meet. While I was studying at Western Reserve University, Dad wanted very much for me to join him in his construction business, which had, by now, grown considerably. My thoughts about working for my dad were mixed. I felt I

315

would never be my own man, and I continued studying at the university.

In 1948, Dad became quite ill and although my family had been in the United States for many years and was totally acclimated, my mother did not trust American doctors. She felt that European doctors, particularly Austrian-trained physicians, were superior and knew more than these "dumb Americans." Although our language and lifestyle was Americanized, my mother's feelings concerning Austrian doctors were deeply rooted. In any event, an Austrian physician was located and upon examining my father, diagnosed him as having had a heart attack. Mark was confined to his room for approximately seven weeks. The doctor's instructions were for him to remain in his upstairs bedroom, in bed, and begin his recuperation.

In the practice of modern medicine, a doctor would allow his patient to continue their lifestyle, albeit with some precautions, and most likely encouraging light exercise. However, my father's doctor did not believe in these methods. Needless to say, this treatment was not the best for Mark. Remaining in a dark and silent room for seven weeks was surely not the modern way to promote my father's healing process. Candidly, I don't believe that Mark ever suffered a heart attack at all. Subsequent checkups in the years to follow revealed no evidence of cardiac damage. This was his second occurrence of medical misdiagnosis, the first having been his experience with exploratory surgery in 1936, and now this treatment based on fear that a life-threatening heart attack had occurred. The consequence of this ailment was my mother's insistence that Mark should retire. In 1948, he was still a young 56 years of age and wanted to continue working. My mother's decision, however, prevailed, and my father retired from his building business.

Having become familiar with Florida during my training in Fort Pierce, my parents decided to spend their winters there to get him away from the harsh Cleveland weather. Dad's retirement years from 1948 up to his death in 1981 were not exciting years for him. Mother and Dad spent their winters in Miami

Beach. I had moved to Miami in 1956 and lived there with my wife and two children, Laurie and Penny. My parents spent each winter from 1948 to 1981 in sunny south Florida. During this very lengthy retirement period, they lived very well on the strength of my father's investments. There was little pension benefit from Social Security. When my father died in 1981, he left a healthy estate that was divided among his three children, after initially reverting to my mother. My mother, Lena, died two years later and the estate was still reasonably sizeable, even after estate taxes were paid. I mention this because it is a strong reflection on Mark's business acumen and success.

During the years following his retirement, Mark didn't know what to do with himself. For a few years, he was an avid reader, but his interest in reading waned as he got older. He became semi-senile in the late 1970's, was increasingly forgetful and had a few minor automobile accidents. He would offer the driver of the other car enough money to cover damages so they would not report the accident to the police. He became a real

Mark and Lena in Bradenton, Florida 1980

danger on the road. Renee, who lived in Cleveland, had her hands full trying to get Mark to stop driving. Eventually she was successful, but it was heartbreaking when they took away his license and sold his car. Now he couldn't get around any more on his own. It was, however, the best thing to do since he had really become an accident waiting to happen. He had for some time been "aiming" his car rather than driving it.

Life was beginning to get burdensome and boring. The many years Mark had worked, made decisions, raised a family and took pride in his accomplishments were not much more than a memory now. The avid reading of years gone by and the interest in everyday activities had waned. Indeed, there was little to which he looked forward. It was breakfast time, then lounging and waiting, and then it was time for lunch. The lounging and waiting and nothing to do took care of most of the afternoon and then it was time for dinner. Life was, indeed, passing both Mark and Lena by, both night and day, day in and day out. The relationship that Lena had with Renee also was deteriorating. This was primarily due to the very boring existence which made her extremely difficult to get along with. She made many demands on Renee that were unreasonable and showed signs of envy for Renee's very active life which exacerbated the situation even more. Matters got to a point where Renee's blood pressure reached 200 and the relationship had deteriorated to where they could not be together on good terms for any length of time. A major change was called for and a move to Florida was suggested.

In 1979, Mark and Lena finally moved permanently to Bradenton, Florida where they lived in their own home which they purchased. They were comfortable, yet lonely and bored with nothing to do as Mother and Dad didn't get involved in anything and found nothing rewarding. Their life was monotonous. Lena had a difficult time with Dad who was now a bit more than semi-senile and it was almost pitiful to see them because there was no purpose to their lives. They were both in their late 80's and knew that their only future was the end.

In early 1981, Mark became both

physically and mentally worse. We took him to the hospital and for the last six months of his life, he lived in a nursing home in Houston, Texas. He was aware of his decline and would often lament, "Look what has happened to me. I've lost my mind; I don't remember anything." There were incidents of incontinence. My father was a vital, proud man, and it pained him to realize that his body and mind had failed him. It was unfair for him to end his days in such a state. I remember him as such a loving and strong man. His demise came on August 6, 1981. At his funeral, there were 200 people who wished to say their last goodbyes to him. He was universally loved and respected by all.

My lovely wife, Marilyn, met Dad when he was 87. She often shaved him and gave him haircuts during the last two years of his life. She was always in love with him and at times seemed in awe of him and has always jestingly said if she had met him first and he were single, there would have been some doubt about who she would have married.

As Mark loved cats in his youth, so does

his grandson, young Mark who was born two months after Grandpa Mark's death. Young Mark loves and adores his two cats in the same way as did Grandpa Mark. Mark, the older, seems to be reincarnated in his grandson Mark. For example, as Mark couldn't even kill a fly, putting a handkerchief over them and taking them outside, young Mark also cannot harm flies, making sure they get out the door he has opened for them. Young Mark also has the same type of "street smarts" as did his grandfather. Genetically, there seems to be one strain that has been passed down from Grandpa Mark to his son Kurt and now to young Mark.

It amazes us to see the love that young Mark has for his grandfather even though they had never met. When young Mark looks at Grandpa Mark's picture, there is almost something eerie in the emotions you can see he feels for his grandfather. To even mention his grandfather to him is to see young Mark light up giving us a feeling of an almost supernatural occurrence.

Indeed, my father, Mark Wallach, was

a wonderful man. His loving kindness could never be forgotten. His deeds of bravery and strength, as he brought his family from their secure and comfortable home in Magdeburg to Holland, and then to America, showed him to be the loving and courageous person that we knew him to be, but never really fully appreciated. He was surely a man of extreme and unusual foresight. Who else could do what he did to take care of those dear to him? I remember Mark Wallach as the most valiant man I have ever known and for the rest of my life will be ever grateful to have been his son. As we look back, we can see my father only as the polished gentleman that he was. My love for him is unbounding, and will always so remain. I see ever so clearly that what we had was indeed the best. I thank him for being, I thank him for the many years during which he was so devoted a father and I thank him for the blessing of life, the opportunity to have known and loved him. His memory will always be on my mind as I live out the rest of my days.

ABOUT THE AUTHOR

Kurt Wallach brings with him a varied background not often found, ranging across a spectrum of a most manifold and wide range of callings, beginning with a short and almost non-existent career as a hearing and speech pathologist. He completed his master's degree studies at Western Reserve University, and many weeks of practice teaching in this field, but never continued toward a career.

Not finding the future lucrative here, he incorporated an aluminum storm window company in Cleveland, Ohio, at the age of 23 and was inordinately successful until he sold it, and moved to Miami, Florida, where he built several subdivisions, apartment complexes, and an office building. He built Florida's first condominium in 1960, subdivided a 1,460 acre piece of land in South Dade County (Miami) and a 2,700 lot subdivision in Stuart, Florida. He patented a lady's hairstyling tool, selling over 19,000,000 pieces, merging his company with another and placing it on the American Stock Exchange before retiring from it.

ABOUT THE AUTHOR

Wallach spent several years as a tennis professional and then built the Miami Racquet Club. It was at this time that he did his first published writing, producing and having published a humorous tennis book called, "Tennis is a Funny Racquet," a book which became quite successful. At the same time he wrote a weekly newspaper column, "Tennis Technique" which was syndicated in numerous magazines and newspapers throughout Florida. He was a frequent umpire at the U.S. Tennis Open as a "chair umpire" working many major nationally televised matches. During this time he became an avid duplicate bridge player participating in many statewide tournaments and achieving the designation of Junior Master from the American Contract Bridge League.

Kurt Wallach later re-entered the real estate industry via some construction and for the past 16 years has been engaged primarily in investments in manufactured housing communities, shopping plazas and other real estate investments including the ownership of a successful mortgage company, land, office building, etc.

ABOUT THE AUTHOR

He is a substantial contributor to the Holocaust Museum. As a major stockholder of Citrus Bank, Mr. Wallach also serves on its board of directors. He has been chairman of several major committees including the chairmanship of the important executive loan committee. He has recently donated 55 acres of land to the State of Florida for the protection of the environment. He is a sponsor of the Indian River Humane Society, a benefactor of the Treasure Coast Opera Society and serves on its board of directors. Mr. Wallach also serves on the board of directors of the Vero Heritage Center. He is the father of two daughters, Laurie Mitchell and Penny Spark, and has a 13 year old son, Mark, who was born two months after his grandfather's death in 1981. A bit of his career in the United States Navy during World War II is found in the book.